Hungry Girl
200 under 200
Just
DESSERTS

Also by Lisa Lillien

Hungry Girl:
Recipes and Survival Strategies for Guilt-Free Eating in the Real World

Hungry Girl 200 Under 200:
200 Recipes Under 200 Calories

Hungry Girl 1-2-3:
The Easiest, Most Delicious, Guilt-Free Recipes on the Planet

Hungry Girl Happy Hour:
75 Recipes for Amazingly Fantastic Guilt-Free Cocktails & Party Foods

Hungry Girl 300 Under 300:
300 Breakfast, Lunch & Dinner Dishes Under 300 Calories

Hungry Girl Supermarket Survival:
Aisle by Aisle, HG-Style!

HUNGRY GIRL TO THE MAX!
The Ultimate Guilt-Free Cookbook

Hungry Girl: The Official Survival Guides:
Tips & Tricks for Guilt-Free Eating
(audio book)

Hungry Girl Chew the Right Thing:
Supreme Makeovers for 50 Foods You Crave
(recipe cards)

Hungry Girl

200 under 200

Just DESSERTS

200 Recipes Under 200 Calories

WITHDRAWN

Lisa Lillien

St. Martin's Griffin

New York

The author's references to various brand-name products and services are for informational purposes only and are not intended to suggest endorsement or sponsorship of the author or her book by any company, organization, or owner of any brand.

HUNGRY GIRL 200 UNDER 200 JUST DESSERTS:
200 RECIPES UNDER 200 CALORIES.
COPYRIGHT © 2013 by Hungry Girl, Inc. All rights reserved. Printed in the United States of America. For information, address St. Martin's Press, 175 Fifth Avenue, New York, N.Y. 10010.

www.stmartins.com

Cover design and book design by Elizabeth Hodson

Illustrations by Jack Pullan

Food styling and photography by General Mills Photography Studios

      Photographer: Val Bourassa

      Food Stylists: Carol Grones and Karen Linden

      Photography Assistant: Kayla Pieper

ISBN 978-0-312-67674-2 {trade paperback}
ISBN 978-1-250-03191-4 {e-book}

First Edition: May 2013

10 9 8 7 6 5 4 3 2 1

CONTENTS

Strawberry Shortcake Cream Fluff Cups
Banana Cream Fluff Cups
Caramel Apple Cream Fluff Cups
Bananas Foster Cream Fluff Cups
Triple Chocolate Cream Fluff Cups
PB&J Surprise Cups
Mini Dutch Apple Pies
Caramel Apple Cream Fluff Stacks
Strawberry Shortcake Cream Fluff Stacks
Berries & Cream Fluff Stacks

CH 13: TRIFLES, PARFAITS & CRÈME BRÛLÉES 296

Rockin' Red Velvet Trifle
Berry-Good Tropical Trifle
Red, White & Blueberry Trifle
Very Cherry Dreamboat Parfaits
Tropical Dreamboat Parfaits
Apple Cinnamon Dreamboat Parfaits
Key Lime Pie-fait
PB 'n Chocolate Puddin' Crunch Parfait
Crunchy Caramel Apple Layer Parfaits
Crème Brûlée Tips 'n Tricks . . .
Cappuccino Crème Brûlée
Coconut Crème Brûlée
Sugar and Spice Crème Brûlée

CH 14: FRUITY FUN 316

Stuffed-Apple Apple Pie
Caramel-Drizzled Caramelized Pineapple
Cherry-Picked Fake-Baked Apple
Craisin'-Amazin' Baked Apples
Raisin' the Roof Baked Apples
Baked Caramel 'n Coconut Apples
Streuseled-Up Baked Peaches
Crazy-Amazing Pineapple Grillers with Coconut Dip
Sugar 'n Spice Baked Pears
Dippy-Good Grilled Fruit Kebabs
Pumpkin-Pie Apple Shakers
Sweet Cinnamon Pear Shakers
Stuffed-with-Love Strawberries
Creamy Dreamy Fruit Fandango

CH 15: DESSERTS IN DISGUISE

Strawberry Shortcake Waffle Tacos
Banana Split Waffle Tacos
Tropical Fruit Waffle Tacos
DIY Choco-Mallow Coconut Nachos
DIY Banana & PB Nachos
DIY Cannoli Nachos
DIY Apple Pie Nachos
Crazy for Caramel Apple Pizza
Sassy S'mores Quesadilla
Pumpkin Pie Pot Stickers
Dreamy PB Chocolate Ravioli Puffs

RECIPES BY CATEGORY

Desserts for One
30 Minutes or Less
5 Ingredients or Less
Chocolate Madness!
Cookies 'n Cream Dream
Red Velvet Revolution
Loco for Choco-Coconut
More & More S'mores
Peanut Butter Passion
Caramel Crazy
Very Vanilla
Say Cheesecake
Fruity & Fabulous
Apple-mania
Strawberry Shortcake Surprise
Bananarama
Tropical Treats
Pumpkin Attack!

INDEX

ACKNOWLEDGMENTS
Tremendous THANK-YOUs are in order!

I'd like to thank the following humans (and animals!) for their help with this book by sharing cute photos of them . . . :)

That's me!

Jamie Goldberg
Managing Editor who got her start in the kitchen VERY early!

Elizabeth Hodson
Now a designer, she was always a CHEWER!

Amanda Pisani
B.P. (Before Proofreading.)

Lisa Friedman
Lisa does it ALL (and is still this cute)!

Daniel Schneider
My amazing husband. (FYI—this pic could have been taken last week!)

Anne Marie Tallberg
Marketer extraordinaire over at St. Martin's Press!

Alison Kreuch
Advertising & Marketing master and lover of candy!

Jennifer Curtis
Master proofreader, since age three!

John Vaccaro
Keeps me sane while looking THAT GOOD in plaid!

Meri Lillien & Jay Lillien
My super-stylish siblings . . . with four-year-old ME!

Jackie Mgido
Hair & makeup superstar. Can't you tell?!

John Karle
PR guru who has since greatly improved his eating skills.

Florence & Maurice Lillien
Hi, Mom & Dad . . . THANKS FOR PUTTING ME HERE!!

Jackson
"Snackson" Jackson!

Jack Pullan
HG artist. He's been at it a long time!

Michelle Ferrand

Fun-loving kitchen queen!

Lynn Bettencourt

Multi-tasking HGer, back in her Boston days!

Callie Pegadiotes

Food stylist/photographer/ birthday-cake enjoyer.

Bill Stankey

My manager . . . What a baby!!!

Samantha Oliver

Editorial wiz/cake fan!

Dana DeRuyck

Editor, recipe developer . . . She STILL enjoys cakes larger than she is! (Who doesn't?!)

Melissa Klotz

Daily-email designer and snazzy fashionista!

Neeti Madan

My literary agent . . . She hasn't changed a bit!

Sarie Solomon

Test-kitchen assistant, nicest human ever, and an excellent driver!

Cupcake

Banana-lovin' bun!

Michelle Weintraub

Marketing maven with exceptional table manners!

Matthew Shear

Publisher at St. Martin's— CUTE BABY, RIGHT?!?!

Tom Fineman

My lovable attorney!

Jennifer Enderlin

St. Martin's Press editorial genius. Voted MOST AWESOME in high school. (She should've been, anyway!)

John Murphy

Publicity pro at St. Martin's. This guy NEVER changes.

Jeff Becker

My business manager rarely goes to work in PJs these days . . . ;)

And special thanks to Nanci Dixon, Cindy Lund, and all the wonderful folks at the General Mills Photography Studios. YOU ROCK SO MUCH!!!

INTRODUCTION

Welcome to *Hungry Girl 200 Under 200 Just Desserts*!
This book is filled with exactly what you think it's filled with—200 desserts with
less than 200 calories each! The original *Hungry Girl 200 Under 200* is one of
my favorite HG books, and I REALLY wanted to expand on that "less than
200 calories" concept. I thought—WOW—why not create an entire book of
recipes for decadent treats and desserts that have under 200 calories each?!
After *chewing* on it for a while (pun intended!), I decided there wasn't a
single reason why this book shouldn't exist—and so here it is. SWEET! I hope
you love it as much as I do . . .

For the newbies out there, Hungry Girl is a lifestyle brand that started
as a free daily email service about guilt-free eating. The emails (read by over
a million people a day) feature news, food finds, recipes, and real-world tips
& survival strategies. Hungry Girl was started by me, Lisa Lillien. I'm not a
doctor or nutrition professional; I'm just hungry! Back in 2004, I decided I wanted
to share my love and knowledge of guilt-free eating with the world, so Hungry
Girl was born. To sign up for the daily emails or to see what you've missed since
the beginning, go to hungry-girl.com.

The Hungry Girl way of eating is a bridge between the average
American junk-food-packed diet and the idealistic way of eating perfectly
healthy foods at all times. It's a realistic approach to better-for-you eating that
people can actually live with and feel good about. HG recipes fulfill real-world
cravings for EVERYTHING—including fattening foods like cheesecake, brownies,
and fudge—without containing a tremendous amount of calories and fat.

The recipes in this book often call for simple supermarket staples, like boxed cake mix. That's so *anyone* can easily make them. Yes, some of these products are processed. Incorporating these ingredients into HG recipes helps cut out the excessive calories and fat in the indulgent desserts you crave. And we believe that eating these things in moderation can help you achieve and maintain a healthy weight.

Maybe the next time you're about to sink your teeth into a Texas-sized frosted cupcake or jab your fork into a mountainous restaurant dessert, you'll think about this book, head home, and whip up one of these desserts instead. Happy chewing!

AWESOME FEATURE ALERT!

Looking for recipes with five ingredients or less, single-serving desserts, or recipes that take 30 minutes or less? Just flip to the Recipes by Category section at the back of the book. Are you a chocoholic? Obsessed with red velvet? Crazy for caramel? There's a section for that too—the Recipes by Flavor, beginning on page 357!

GET THE PHOTOS AND *POINTSPLUS*® VALUES FOR ALL 200 RECIPES!

Not every single recipe is lucky enough to have a photo here, so we've captured each and every one for your online viewing pleasure! And since we're big fans of Weight Watchers (and know many of you are too!), we've calculated the Weight Watchers *PointsPlus*® values* for all of the recipes in *Hungry Girl 200 Under 200 Just Desserts* and put them on our website.

Visit hungry-girl.com/books for the photos and values!

*The PointsPlus® values for these recipes were calculated by Hungry Girl and are not an endorsement or approval of the recipe or developer by Weight Watchers International, Inc., the owner of the PointsPlus® registered trademark.

KITCHEN ESSENTIALS

A few must-haves for guilt-free dessert making . . .

STOVETOP COOKWARE:
small, medium, and large nonstick pots

BAKING NEEDS:
a couple of baking sheets, a 9-inch pie pan, a 9-inch round cake pan, a 9-inch springform cake pan, an 8-inch by 8-inch baking pan, a 9-inch by 13-inch baking pan, a 12-cup muffin pan, and foil cupcake liners

MICROWAVE-SAFE ESSENTIALS:
bowls and mugs

MEASURING MUST-HAVES:
spoons, cups (including a liquid measuring cup), and a kitchen scale

COUNTERTOP TOOLS:
a blender or food processor, a cooling rack, an electric mixer, a whisk, mixing bowls, rubber spatulas (optional, but helpful), and a rolling pin (optional)

RECOMMENDED PRODUCTS

Some brands are better than others, and we're naming names!

FAT-FREE GREEK YOGURT
Fage Total 0%, Chobani 0%

FAT-FREE LIQUID EGG SUBSTITUTE
Egg Beaters Original, Better'n Eggs

FAT-FREE CREAM CHEESE (IN A TUB)
Philadelphia Fat Free

LIGHT SOYMILK
8th Continent Light, Silk Light

LIGHT BUTTERY SPREAD AND LIGHT WHIPPED BUTTER IN A TUB
Brummel & Brown, Land O Lakes
    Whipped Light, Smart Balance Light

SUGAR-FREE PUDDING CUPS WITH 60 CALORIES OR LESS (REFRIGERATED OR SHELF STABLE)
Jell-O Sugar Free, Snack Pack Sugar Free

SUGAR-FREE POWDERED CREAMER
Coffee-mate Sugar Free

OLD-FASHIONED OATS
Old Fashioned Quaker Oats

CANNED PURE PUMPKIN (NOT PUMPKIN PIE MIX!)
Libby's 100%

RICE CAKES AND MINI RICE CAKES
Quaker

GRAHAM CRACKERS
Honey Maid

MINI MARSHMALLOWS
Jet-Puffed Mini

FROZEN LOW-FAT WAFFLES
Eggo Low Fat, Van's Lite

LIGHT AND FAT-FREE ICE CREAM
Dreyer's/Edy's Slow Churned,
    Breyers Fat Free

FROZEN MINI FILLO SHELLS
Athens

CREAMY REDUCED-FAT PEANUT BUTTER
Skippy Reduced Fat Creamy

RECOMMENDED PRODUCTS

POWDERED PEANUT BUTTER
(SEE PAGE 8 FOR MORE INFO!)

PB2, FitNutz

LOW-SUGAR FRUIT PRESERVES

Smucker's Low Sugar

FAT-FREE, LOW-FAT, OR LIGHT CARAMEL DIP (OFTEN FOUND IN THE PRODUCE AISLE)

Marzetti Fat Free and Light, Litehouse Low Fat

LIGHT CHOCOLATE SYRUP

Hershey's Lite

HOT COCOA PACKETS WITH 20 TO 25 CALORIES EACH

Swiss Miss Diet, Nestlé Fat Free

MOIST-STYLE CAKE MIXES

Betty Crocker, Pillsbury

NONSTICK COOKING SPRAY

Pam

NO-CALORIE SWEETENER PACKETS

Splenda, Truvia, Nectresse, Pure Via, Stevia In The Raw

INGREDIENT TIPS 'N TRICKS

DESSERT STORAGE 101 . . .

Any dessert topping made with dairy (such as pudding or cream cheese) needs to be refrigerated. Pies and other desserts made with dairy should also be stored in the fridge.

SWEETENER SWAPPIN'!
The 411 on Sugar Alternatives and No-Calorie Sweetener Alternatives

✱ Some HG desserts call for Splenda No Calorie Sweetener (granulated) because it has around 90 percent fewer calories than sugar. We use real sugar in recipes when not much sweetener is needed or when the taste of real sugar makes a big difference.

✱ Prefer one or the other across the board? There are nutritional stats for every recipe if made with the alternative! Just use the exact same amount when swapping sweeteners. The only recipes without the alternative stats are those in which using real sugar would push the calorie count over 200.

✱ Wanna use natural no-calorie sweeteners in these recipes? Look for products that measure cup-for-cup like real sugar, not packeted products (which are generally much sweeter than sugar).

INGREDIENT TIPS 'N TRICKS

THE POWDERED PB NEED-TO-KNOW . . .

What is it?
Defatted peanuts, finely ground into powder. Each tablespoon has around 25 calories and less than a gram of fat. Mixed with a little water, it doubles as peanut butter. Wow!

Who makes it?
Companies like Bell Plantation (PB2) and FitNutz.

Where is it sold?
Your best bet is to order some online, since it's not easily found in stores. Check out bellplantation.com and fitnutzbutter.com.

Which recipes in this book are made with powdered peanut butter?
The PB Cheesecake Chocolate Cupcakes (page 44), PB & Chocolate Chilly Whoopie Pie (page 191), and Freezy PB S'mores Sandwich (page 200)!

EGG SUBSTITUTE SWAPPIN':
EGG WHITE CONVERSION CHART

You can easily use egg whites in place of fat-free liquid egg substitute. If you buy packaged liquid egg whites, just use an equal amount. If you use actual eggs, refer to this handy chart to get started, but still measure out the amounts . . .

> 2 tablespoons fat-free liquid egg substitute = about 1 large egg white
>
> 1/4 cup fat-free liquid egg substitute = about 2 large egg whites
>
> 1/3 cup fat-free liquid egg substitute = about 3 large egg whites
>
> 1/2 cup fat-free liquid egg substitute = about 4 large egg whites
>
> 1 cup fat-free liquid egg substitute = about 8 large egg whites

INGREDIENT TIPS 'N TRICKS

CARAMEL DIP TIPS!

* Find tubs of the gooey goody in the produce section—usually near the apples. Why? It's often marketed as a fruit dip and is sometimes labeled "Caramel Apple Dip."

* We call for fat-free, low-fat, or light caramel dip, which has around 100 calories per 2-tablespoon serving. If you only see standard caramel dips, don't despair—check the stats. Sometimes their calorie counts are very similar to the light kinds.

SOYMILK SWAP-A-RAMA!

We call for light vanilla soymilk because it's sweet and creamy with fewer calories than regular milk (even the fat-free kind)—a cup of light vanilla soymilk has about 70 calories and 2g fat. But if you avoid soy, there are swaps . . .

Blue Diamond Unsweetened Vanilla Almond Breeze - This stuff has 40 calories and 3.5g fat per cup, and it tastes AMAZING, so it's a great calorie saver! Light vanilla soymilk and Unsweetened Vanilla Almond Breeze are basically interchangeable. If you go with another almond milk, just check the nutritional info before you buy.

So Delicious Unsweetened Coconut Milk Beverage - This is nothing like the "lite coconut milk" that comes in a can! A cup has 50 calories and 5g fat, and the flavor is mild and creamy.

Fat-Free Dairy Milk - This isn't our favorite, but it'll do the trick. A cup has around 80 calories—it'll save you some fat, but it isn't as creamy as the others. Try adding a drop or two of vanilla extract and a no-calorie sweetener packet to amp up the flavor.

CHAPTER 1

CAKE MUGS & MORE DESSERTS IN A MUG

Portion control is KEY when it comes to desserts. So making sweet stuff in individual cups is GENIUS. For those of you who have trouble keeping your dessert portions in check, this MUG's for you . . .

CAKE MUG 411 . . .

✳ Use a standard 12-ounce coffee mug for these recipes.

✳ You can eat your cake right out of the mug, if you like. Just know that popping it out when it's still warm will give your cake a better texture.

✳ It takes about 15 minutes for your mug-made cake to cool. Letting it cool completely gives you more delicious results.

Salted Caramel Chocolate Cake Mug

You'll Need: microwave-safe mug, nonstick spray, plate

Prep: 5 minutes **Cook:** 5 minutes **Cool:** 15 minutes

Entire recipe: 168 calories, 2.5g fat, 650mg sodium, 33g carbs, 1g fiber, 18.5g sugars, 4g protein

Ingredients

3 tablespoons moist-style devil's food cake mix
1 tablespoon fat-free liquid egg substitute
1 tablespoon fat-free sour cream
⅛ teaspoon baking powder
2 tablespoons Fat Free Reddi-wip
1½ teaspoons fat-free, low-fat, or light caramel dip
2 dashes coarse sea salt

Directions

In a microwave-safe mug sprayed with nonstick spray, combine cake mix, egg substitute, sour cream, and baking powder. Add 2 tablespoons water, and mix until uniform.

Microwave for 1 minute and 45 seconds, or until set.

Immediately run a knife along the edges to help separate the cake from the mug. Firmly place a plate over the mug, and flip so that the plate is on the bottom. Gently shake mug to release cake onto the plate.

Let cool completely, about 15 minutes.

Top cake with Reddi-wip, drizzle with caramel, and sprinkle with salt. Eat up!

MAKES 1 SERVING

Chunky Monkey Cake Mug

You'll Need: microwave-safe mug, nonstick spray, plate

Prep: 5 minutes   **Cook:** 5 minutes   **Cool:** 15 minutes

Entire recipe: 190 calories, 4g fat, 366mg sodium, 35.5g carbs, 2g fiber, 19.5g sugars, 4.5g protein

Ingredients

3 tablespoons moist-style devil's food cake mix
1 tablespoon fat-free liquid egg substitute
1 tablespoon fat-free sour cream
⅛ teaspoon baking powder
¼ cup chopped banana
2 tablespoons Fat Free Reddi-wip
1 teaspoon chopped walnuts

Directions

In a microwave-safe mug sprayed with nonstick spray, combine cake mix, egg substitute, sour cream, and baking powder. Add 2 tablespoons water, and mix until uniform. Stir in 2 tablespoons banana.

Microwave for 1 minute and 45 seconds, or until set.

Immediately run a knife along the edges to help separate the cake from the mug. Firmly place a plate over the mug, and flip so that the plate is on the bottom. Gently shake mug to release cake onto the plate.

Let cool completely, about 15 minutes.

Top cake with remaining 2 tablespoons banana. Top with Reddi-wip, and sprinkle with walnuts. Mmmm!

MAKES 1 SERVING

For a pic of this recipe, see the first photo insert. Yay!

So S'mores Cake Mug

You'll Need: microwave-safe mug, nonstick spray, plate

Prep: 5 minutes   **Cook:** 5 minutes   **Cool:** 15 minutes

Entire recipe: 173 calories, 2.5g fat, 397mg sodium, 34g carbs, 1g fiber, 19g sugars, 4g protein

Ingredients

3 tablespoons moist-style devil's food cake mix
1 tablespoon fat-free liquid egg substitute
1 tablespoon fat-free sour cream
⅛ teaspoon baking powder
1 tablespoon Jet-Puffed Marshmallow Creme
1 low-fat honey graham cracker (¼th of a sheet), roughly crushed

Directions

In a microwave-safe mug sprayed with nonstick spray, combine cake mix, egg substitute, sour cream, and baking powder. Add 2 tablespoons water, and mix until uniform.

Microwave for 1 minute and 45 seconds, or until set.

Immediately run a knife along the edges to help separate the cake from the mug. Firmly place a plate over the mug, and flip so that the plate is on the bottom. Gently shake mug to release cake onto the plate.

Let cool completely, about 15 minutes.

Top cake with marshmallow creme, and sprinkle with crushed graham cracker. Dig in!

MAKES 1 SERVING

Gooey German
Chocolate Cake Mug

You'll Need: microwave-safe mug, nonstick spray, plate

Prep: 5 minutes   **Cook:** 5 minutes   **Cool:** 15 minutes

Entire recipe: 194 calories, 6g fat, 398mg sodium, 32.5g carbs, 1.5g fiber, 18g sugars, 4g protein

Ingredients

3 tablespoons moist-style devil's food cake mix
1 tablespoon fat-free liquid egg substitute
1 tablespoon fat-free sour cream
⅛ teaspoon baking powder
1 teaspoon fat-free, low-fat, or light caramel dip
1½ teaspoons finely chopped pecans
1½ teaspoons shredded sweetened coconut, chopped

Directions

In a microwave-safe mug sprayed with nonstick spray, combine cake mix, egg substitute, sour cream, and baking powder. Add 2 tablespoons water, and mix until uniform.

Microwave for 1 minute and 45 seconds, or until set.

Immediately run a knife along the edges to help separate the cake from the mug. Firmly place a plate over the mug, and flip so that the plate is on the bottom. Gently shake mug to release cake onto the plate.

Let cool completely, about 15 minutes.

Drizzle cake with caramel, and sprinkle with pecans and chopped coconut. So good!

MAKES 1 SERVING

Coffee Cake in a Mug

You'll Need: sealable plastic bag, meat mallet or heavy utensil, small bowl, microwave-safe mug, nonstick spray

Prep: 5 minutes   **Cook:** 5 minutes

Entire recipe: 156 calories, 3g fat, 375mg sodium, 33g carbs, 2g fiber, 18.5g sugars, 1g protein

Ingredients

1 tablespoon Fiber One Original bran cereal
2 teaspoons brown sugar (not packed)
¼ teaspoon plus 1 dash cinnamon
½ teaspoon light whipped butter or light buttery spread
3 tablespoons moist-style yellow cake mix
3 tablespoons club soda
1 drop almond extract
¼ teaspoon baking powder

Directions

Place cereal in a sealable plastic bag and, using a meat mallet or heavy utensil, crush into crumbs.

Transfer crumbs to a small bowl. Mix in brown sugar and ¼ teaspoon cinnamon. Add butter, and mash and stir until well mixed and crumbly.

In a microwave-safe mug sprayed with nonstick spray, combine cake mix, club soda, almond extract, baking powder, and remaining dash cinnamon. Stir until uniform.

Sprinkle crumb mixture over the cake mixture. Microwave for 1 minute and 45 seconds, or until set. Enjoy straight from the mug!

MAKES 1 SERVING

Perfect Piña Colada Cake Mug

You'll Need: medium bowl, microwave-safe mug, nonstick spray, plate

Prep: 5 minutes   **Cook:** 5 minutes   **Cool:** 15 minutes

Entire recipe: 187 calories, 4.5g fat, 345mg sodium, 33.5g carbs, 1.5g fiber, 19.5g sugars, 3.5g protein

Ingredients

3 tablespoons moist-style yellow cake mix
1 tablespoon fat-free liquid egg substitute
1 tablespoon fat-free sour cream
⅛ teaspoon baking powder
1 drop coconut extract
1 tablespoon shredded sweetened coconut
1½ tablespoons crushed pineapple packed in juice (not drained)
2 tablespoons Fat Free Reddi-wip

Directions

In a medium bowl, combine cake mix, egg substitute, sour cream, baking powder, and coconut extract. Add 2 teaspoons shredded coconut and 2 tablespoons water. Mix until uniform.

Spray a microwave-safe mug with nonstick spray. Add undrained pineapple, and top with cake mixture. Do not stir.

Microwave for 1 minute and 45 seconds, or until set.

Immediately run a knife along the edges to help separate the cake from the mug. Firmly place a plate over the mug, and flip so that the plate is on the bottom. Gently shake mug to release cake onto the plate.

Let cool completely, about 15 minutes.

Top cake with Reddi-wip and remaining teaspoon coconut. Mmmm!

MAKES 1 SERVING

187 calories per serving

Strawberry Shortcake in a Mug

You'll Need: microwave-safe mug, nonstick spray, plate, small bowl

Prep: 5 minutes   **Cook:** 5 minutes   **Cool:** 15 minutes

Entire recipe: 173 calories, 2.5g fat, 326mg sodium, 34g carbs, 0.5g fiber, 19g sugars, 3g protein

Ingredients

3 tablespoons moist-style yellow cake mix
1 tablespoon fat-free liquid egg substitute
1 tablespoon fat-free sour cream
⅛ teaspoon baking powder
2 tablespoons chopped strawberries
2 teaspoons low-sugar strawberry preserves
2 tablespoons Cool Whip Free (thawed)

Directions

In a microwave-safe mug sprayed with nonstick spray, combine cake mix, egg substitute, sour cream, and baking powder. Add 2 tablespoons water, and mix until uniform.

Microwave for 1 minute and 45 seconds, or until set.

Immediately run a knife along the edges to help separate the cake from the mug. Firmly place a plate over the mug, and flip so that the plate is on the bottom. Gently shake mug to release cake onto the plate.

Let cool completely, about 15 minutes.

In a small bowl, mix strawberries with preserves.

Top cake with strawberry mixture, followed by Cool Whip. Yum!

MAKES 1 SERVING

173 calories per serving

For more recipes, tips & tricks, sign up for FREE daily emails at **hungry-girl.com!**

Oreo Cheesecake in a Mug

You'll Need: mug

Prep: 5 minutes **Chill:** 20 minutes

Entire recipe: 171 calories, 2.5g fat, 498mg sodium, 24g carbs, 0.5g fiber, 9.5g sugars, 11g protein

Ingredients

½ pack Nabisco 100 Cal Oreo Thin Crisps
¼ cup fat-free ricotta cheese
2 tablespoons fat-free cream cheese
1 no-calorie sweetener packet
½ tablespoon Jell-O Sugar Free Fat Free Vanilla Instant pudding mix
⅛ teaspoon vanilla extract
¼ cup Cool Whip Free (thawed)

Optional topping: Fat Free Reddi-wip

HG Alternative: *No Oreo Thin Crisps? Just use 3 chocolate graham crackers (¾ sheet) instead.*

Directions

Break half of the cookies into small pieces, and finely crush the other half.

In a mug, combine ricotta cheese, cream cheese, sweetener, pudding mix, and vanilla extract. Vigorously stir until uniform. Fold in Cool Whip until uniform, and gently stir in the cookies that have been broken into small pieces. Cover and refrigerate until thickened, at least 20 minutes.

Top with the finely crushed cookies. Dig in!

MAKES 1 SERVING

Apple Crisp in a Mug

You'll Need: small microwave-safe bowl, large microwave-safe mug, nonstick spray

Prep: 5 minutes   **Cook:** 5 minutes

> **Entire recipe:** 178 calories, 1.5g fat, 171mg sodium, 41g carbs, 4g fiber, 27g sugars, 2g protein

Ingredients

1 tablespoon old-fashioned oats
½ teaspoon light whipped butter or light buttery spread
Dash nutmeg
Dash salt
1 tablespoon brown sugar (not packed)
1 tablespoon whole-wheat flour
¼ teaspoon plus 1 dash cinnamon
1½ cups peeled and chopped Fuji apples

Optional topping: Fat Free Reddi-wip

Directions

In a small microwave-safe bowl, combine oats, butter, nutmeg, and salt. Add 2 teaspoons brown sugar, 1 teaspoon flour, and a dash of cinnamon. Mash and stir until well mixed and crumbly. Microwave for 30 seconds, or until firm.

Place apples in a large microwave-safe mug sprayed with nonstick spray. Sprinkle with remaining 1 teaspoon brown sugar, 2 teaspoons flour, and ¼ teaspoon cinnamon. Stir to coat. Microwave for 4 minutes, or until apples are tender.

Stir oat mixture, breaking it into pieces, and sprinkle it over the apple mixture. Mmmm!

MAKES 1 SERVING

Blueberry Crisp in a Mug

You'll Need: small microwave-safe bowl, large microwave-safe mug, nonstick spray

Prep: 5 minutes   **Cook:** 5 minutes

Entire recipe: 185 calories, 2g fat, 173mg sodium, 42g carbs, 6g fiber, 26g sugars, 2g protein

Ingredients

1 tablespoon old-fashioned oats
½ teaspoon light whipped butter or light buttery spread
Dash salt
1 tablespoon brown sugar (not packed)
1 tablespoon whole-wheat flour
¼ teaspoon plus 1 dash cinnamon
1¼ cups frozen unsweetened blueberries, thawed and drained

Optional topping: Fat Free Reddi-wip

Directions

In a small microwave-safe bowl, combine oats, butter, and salt. Add 2 teaspoons brown sugar, 1 teaspoon flour, and a dash of cinnamon. Mash and stir until well mixed and crumbly. Microwave for 30 seconds, or until firm.

Place blueberries in a large microwave-safe mug sprayed with nonstick spray. Sprinkle with remaining 1 teaspoon brown sugar, 2 teaspoons flour, and ¼ teaspoon cinnamon. Stir to coat. Microwave for 1½ minutes, or until hot.

Stir oat mixture, breaking it into pieces, and sprinkle it over the blueberry mixture. Dig in!

MAKES 1 SERVING

Peach Crisp in a Mug

You'll Need: small microwave-safe bowl, large microwave-safe mug, nonstick spray

Prep: 5 minutes   **Cook:** 5 minutes

Entire recipe: 196 calories, 1.5g fat, 170mg sodium, 46.5g carbs, 5.5g fiber, 30g sugars, 3.5g protein

Ingredients

1 tablespoon old-fashioned oats
½ teaspoon light whipped butter or light buttery spread
Dash nutmeg
Dash salt
1 tablespoon brown sugar (not packed)
1 tablespoon whole-wheat flour
¼ teaspoon plus 1 dash cinnamon
1 ¾ cups frozen unsweetened peach slices, thawed, drained, chopped

Optional topping: Fat Free Reddi-wip

Directions

In a small microwave-safe bowl, combine oats, butter, nutmeg, and salt. Add 2 teaspoons brown sugar, 1 teaspoon flour, and a dash of cinnamon. Mash and stir until well mixed and crumbly. Microwave for 30 seconds, or until firm.

Place peaches in a large microwave-safe mug sprayed with nonstick spray. Sprinkle with remaining 1 teaspoon brown sugar, 2 teaspoons flour, and ¼ teaspoon cinnamon. Stir to coat. Microwave for 1 ½ minutes, or until hot.

Stir oat mixture, breaking it into pieces, and sprinkle it over the peach mixture. Eat up!

MAKES 1 SERVING

For a pic of this recipe, see the first photo insert. Yay!

196 calories per serving

Streusel-Topped Pumpkin Pie in a Mug

You'll Need: mug, small microwave-safe bowl

Prep: 5 minutes   **Cook:** 5 minutes   **Chill:** 30 minutes

Entire recipe: 147 calories, 1g fat, 407mg sodium, 31g carbs, 7g fiber, 12.5g sugars, 3g protein

Ingredients

1 tablespoon Jell-O Sugar Free Fat Free Vanilla Instant pudding mix
⅔ cup canned pure pumpkin
⅛ teaspoon pumpkin pie spice
1 no-calorie sweetener packet
2½ teaspoons brown sugar (not packed)
⅛ teaspoon plus 1 dash cinnamon
1 tablespoon old-fashioned oats
1 teaspoon whole-wheat flour
½ teaspoon light whipped butter or light buttery spread
Dash salt

Optional topping: Fat Free Reddi-wip

Directions

Place pudding mix in a mug. Add 2 tablespoons cold water, and vigorously stir until mostly smooth and slightly thickened. Add pumpkin, pumpkin pie spice, sweetener, ½ teaspoon brown sugar, and ⅛ teaspoon cinnamon. Mix until uniform. Cover and refrigerate until chilled, about 30 minutes.

For a pic of this recipe, see the first photo insert. Yay!

Meanwhile, in a small microwave-safe bowl, combine oats, flour, butter, and salt. Add remaining 2 teaspoons brown sugar and dash of cinnamon. Mash and stir until well mixed and crumbly. Microwave for 30 seconds, or until firm.

Stir oat mixture, breaking it into pieces, and sprinkle it over the pumpkin mixture. Enjoy!

MAKES 1 SERVING

147 calories per serving

Hungry for More?

Flip to page 351 for ALL the single-serving desserts!

CHAPTER 2

CUPCAKES

Trendy or not, cupcakes are ALWAYS a crowd-pleaser. Try to find a person who doesn't smile when they come face-to-face with a cupcake. Try it! You'll fail. (And yes, smarty-pants . . . we know that cupcakes typically don't have faces.)

CUPCAKE CLASS IS NOW IN SESSION...

Cupcake Cooling 101:
For best results, use a cooling rack. No rack? Use a plate!

Longing for super-cute foil baking cups?
Check your local craft store. You can also find lots of them online!

Pipe Out!
Make your cupcakes look extra schmancy—use a piping bag to distribute your icing or frosting mixture. Find piping kits at places like Target, Walmart, and Bed Bath & Beyond. Or create your own makeshift piping bag! Just transfer your dessert topping to a plastic bag, and squeeze it down toward a bottom corner. Snip off that corner with scissors, creating a small hole for piping. Ta-da!

Mixing up a small amount of icing?
Use a narrow spoon handle instead of the spoon end. It just works better, especially for sticky ingredients.

Snickers-licious Cupcakes

You'll Need: 12-cup muffin pan, foil baking cups or nonstick spray, large bowl, whisk

Prep: 15 minutes   **Cook:** 20 minutes   **Cool:** 25 minutes

> **1/12th of recipe (1 cupcake):** 137 calories, 4g fat, 271mg sodium, 24g carbs, 1g fiber, 14g sugars, 2.5g protein

137 calories per serving

Ingredients

1 ¾ cups moist-style devil's food cake mix
½ cup fat-free liquid egg substitute
¾ teaspoon baking powder
¼ cup mini semi-sweet chocolate chips
2 tablespoons fat-free, low-fat, or light caramel dip
2 tablespoons chopped peanuts

Directions

Preheat oven to 350 degrees. Line a 12-cup muffin pan with foil baking cups, or spray it with nonstick spray.

In a large bowl, combine cake mix, egg substitute, and baking powder. Add 1 cup water, and whisk until smooth.

Evenly distribute batter among the cups of the muffin pan.

Sprinkle with 2 tablespoons chocolate chips. Bake until a toothpick inserted into the center of a cupcake comes out clean, 16 to 18 minutes.

Let cool completely, about 10 minutes in the pan and 15 minutes out of the pan.

Spread cupcakes with caramel dip. Sprinkle with peanuts and remaining 2 tablespoons chocolate chips. Devour!

MAKES 12 SERVINGS

Rockin' Rocky Road Cupcakes

You'll Need: 12-cup muffin pan, foil baking cups or nonstick spray, large bowl, whisk, small bowl

Prep: 15 minutes   **Cook:** 20 minutes   **Cool:** 25 minutes

1/12th of recipe (1 cupcake): 148 calories, 4.5g fat, 256mg sodium, 25g carbs, 1g fiber, 15g sugars, 3g protein

Ingredients

1¾ cups moist-style devil's food cake mix
½ cup fat-free liquid egg substitute
¾ teaspoon baking powder
¼ cup unsalted roasted almonds, roughly chopped
¼ cup Jet-Puffed Marshmallow Creme
1 teaspoon light vanilla soymilk
¼ cup mini semi-sweet chocolate chips
36 mini marshmallows

HG Alternative: Feel free to use milk or your milk swap of choice in place of the soymilk. It'll barely affect the taste or nutritionals.

Directions

Preheat oven to 350 degrees. Line a 12-cup muffin pan with foil baking cups, or spray it with nonstick spray.

In a large bowl, combine cake mix, egg substitute, and baking powder. Add 1 cup water, and whisk until smooth.

Stir in chopped almonds. Evenly distribute batter among the cups of the muffin pan.

Bake until a toothpick inserted into the center of a cupcake comes out clean, 16 to 18 minutes.

Let cool completely, about 10 minutes in the pan and 15 minutes out of the pan.

In a small bowl, mix marshmallow creme with soymilk until uniform. Drizzle over cupcakes.

Sprinkle cupcakes with chocolate chips, and top each cupcake with 3 mini marshmallows. Enjoy!

MAKES 12 SERVINGS

148 calories per serving

✳ Flip to the photo inserts to see dozens of recipe pics! And for photos of ALL the recipes, go to **hungry-girl.com/books**.

S'mores Cupcakes

You'll Need: 12-cup muffin pan, foil baking cups or nonstick spray, large bowl, whisk, small bowl

Prep: 15 minutes   **Cook:** 20 minutes   **Cool:** 25 minutes

1/12th of recipe (1 cupcake): 123 calories, 2.5g fat, 264mg sodium, 24g carbs, 0.5g fiber, 14g sugars, 2.5g protein

Ingredients

1¾ cups moist-style devil's food cake mix
½ cup fat-free liquid egg substitute
¾ teaspoon baking powder
¼ cup Jet-Puffed Marshmallow Creme
1 teaspoon light vanilla soymilk
1 sheet (4 crackers) low-fat honey graham crackers, roughly crushed
2 tablespoons mini semi-sweet chocolate chips
36 mini marshmallows

HG Alternative: Feel free to use milk or your milk swap of choice in place of the soymilk. It'll barely affect the taste or nutritionals.

Directions

Preheat oven to 350 degrees. Line a 12-cup muffin pan with foil baking cups, or spray it with nonstick spray.

In a large bowl, combine cake mix, egg substitute, and baking powder. Add 1 cup water, and whisk until smooth.

Evenly distribute batter among the cups of the muffin pan.

Bake until a toothpick inserted into the center of a cupcake comes out clean, 16 to 18 minutes.

Let cool completely, about 10 minutes in the pan and 15 minutes out of the pan.

In a small bowl, mix marshmallow creme with soymilk until uniform.

Drizzle cupcakes with marshmallow creme mixture. Sprinkle with crushed graham crackers and chocolate chips. Top each cupcake with 3 mini marshmallows, and enjoy!

MAKES 12 SERVINGS

123 calories per serving

For more recipes, tips & tricks, sign up for FREE daily emails at **hungry-girl.com!**

Black Forest Cupcakes

You'll Need: 12-cup muffin pan, foil baking cups or nonstick spray, small nonstick pot, medium bowl, large bowl, whisk

Prep: 15 minutes   **Cook:** 40 minutes   **Cool:** 25 minutes

1/12th of recipe (1 cupcake): 134 calories, 2.5g fat, 266mg sodium, 25.5g carbs, 1g fiber, 15.5g sugars, 2.5g protein

Ingredients

1 tablespoon cornstarch
1½ cups frozen unsweetened pitted
    dark sweet cherries
1½ tablespoons granulated white sugar
Dash salt
1¾ cups moist-style devil's food cake mix
½ cup fat-free liquid egg substitute
¾ teaspoon baking powder
3 tablespoons mini semi-sweet chocolate chips

**No-Calorie
Sweetener Alternative:**

129 calories, 24.5g carbs,
14g sugars

Directions

Preheat oven to 350 degrees. Line a 12-cup muffin pan with foil baking cups, or spray it with nonstick spray.

In a small nonstick pot, combine cornstarch with ⅓ cup cold water, and stir to dissolve. Add cherries, sugar, and salt, and mix well.

Set heat to medium. Stirring frequently, cook until thick and gooey, 16 to 18 minutes.

Transfer to a medium bowl.

In a large bowl, combine cake mix, egg substitute, and baking powder. Add 1 cup water, and whisk until smooth.

Evenly distribute batter among the cups of the muffin pan.

Bake until a toothpick inserted into the center of a cupcake comes out clean, 16 to 18 minutes.

Let cool completely, about 10 minutes in the pan and 15 minutes out of the pan.

Evenly distribute cherry mixture among the cupcakes, and sprinkle with chocolate chips. Eat up!

MAKES 12 SERVINGS

134 calories per serving

Boston Cream Cupcakes

You'll Need: 12-cup muffin pan, foil baking cups or nonstick spray, small bowl, large bowl, whisk, sealable plastic bag

Prep: 20 minutes   **Cook:** 20 minutes   **Cool:** 25 minutes

1/12th of recipe (1 cupcake): 117 calories, 2.5g fat, 213mg sodium, 22g carbs, 0g fiber, 12g sugars, 2g protein

Ingredients

3 tablespoons chocolate frosting
1 tablespoon light chocolate syrup
1 ¾ cups moist-style yellow cake mix
½ cup fat-free liquid egg substitute
¼ teaspoon vanilla extract
1 no-calorie sweetener packet
One sugar-free vanilla pudding snack with 60 calories or less

Directions

Preheat oven to 350 degrees. Line a 12-cup muffin pan with foil baking cups, or spray it with nonstick spray.

In a small bowl, mix frosting with syrup until smooth and uniform. Cover and refrigerate.

In a large bowl, combine cake mix with egg substitute. Add ½ cup water, and whisk until smooth.

Evenly distribute batter among the cups of the muffin pan.

Bake until a toothpick inserted into the center of a cupcake comes out clean, 16 to 18 minutes.

Let cool completely, about 10 minutes in the pan and 15 minutes out of the pan.

Use a knife or narrow spoon handle to create a centered hole through the top of each cupcake, stopping about midway through.

Stir vanilla extract and sweetener into the pudding. Place mixture in one of the bottom corners of a sealable plastic bag. Remove air and seal. Snip off a small part of that corner with scissors.

Gently squeeze the bag and evenly pipe pudding through the hole in the bag's corner and into the holes in the cupcakes.

Evenly spread frosting mixture over the cupcakes. (Don't worry if some of the pudding filling gets mixed in!)

Serve and enjoy!

MAKES 12 SERVINGS

117 calories per serving

Mudslide Cupcakes

You'll Need: 12-cup muffin pan, foil baking cups or nonstick spray, medium bowl, glass, large bowl, whisk

Prep: 20 minutes   **Cook:** 20 minutes   **Cool:** 25 minutes

1/12th of recipe (1 cupcake): 147 calories, 3.5g fat, 303mg sodium, 27g carbs, 1g fiber, 15g sugars, 2.5g protein

Ingredients

⅓ cup chocolate frosting
1 sugar-free chocolate pudding snack with 60 calories or less
1 tablespoon mini semi-sweet chocolate chips
1 tablespoon plus 1 teaspoon instant coffee granules
1¾ cups moist-style devil's food cake mix
½ cup fat-free liquid egg substitute
¾ teaspoon baking powder
2 sheets (8 crackers) chocolate graham crackers, roughly crushed

Directions

Preheat oven to 350 degrees. Line a 12-cup muffin pan with foil baking cups, or spray it with nonstick spray.

In a medium bowl, mix frosting with pudding until smooth and uniform. Cover and refrigerate.

Place chocolate chips and coffee granules in a glass. Add ¼ cup very hot water, and stir until mostly dissolved. Add ¾ cup cold water.

Transfer chocolate-coffee mixture to a large bowl. Add cake mix, egg substitute, and baking powder. Whisk until smooth.

Evenly distribute batter among the cups of the muffin pan.

Bake until a toothpick inserted into the center of a cupcake comes out clean, 16 to 18 minutes.

Let cool completely, about 10 minutes in the pan and 15 minutes out of the pan.

Spread cupcakes with frosting mixture, and sprinkle with crushed grahams. Eat!

MAKES 12 SERVINGS

Hungry for More?

For more coffee creations, check out the **Vanilla Latte Cupcakes** (page 62), **Scoopy Mocha-Coconut Cream Pie** (page 156), **Mochaccino Cream Fluff Cups** (page 274), and **Cappuccino Crème Brûlée** (page 310)!

Double-Decker Fudgy Cheesecake Cupcakes

You'll Need: 12-cup muffin pan, foil baking cups, medium-large bowl, electric mixer, large bowl, whisk

Prep: 15 minutes   **Cook:** 25 minutes   **Cool:** 40 minutes

1/12th of recipe (1 cupcake): 159 calories, 4.5g fat, 337mg sodium, 26g carbs, 1g fiber, 15.5g sugars, 4g protein

Ingredients

One 8-ounce tub fat-free cream cheese
¼ cup fat-free liquid egg substitute
⅓ cup Splenda No Calorie
      Sweetener (granulated)
1 drop vanilla extract
1¾ cups moist-style devil's food cake mix
¾ cup club soda
½ cup mini semi-sweet chocolate chips

Sugar Alternative:

178 calories, 31g carbs,
21g sugars

Directions

Preheat oven to 350 degrees. Line a 12-cup muffin pan with foil baking cups.

Place cream cheese in a medium-large bowl. With an electric mixer set to medium speed, beat until smooth. Add egg substitute, Splenda, and vanilla extract. Beat until smooth.

In a large bowl, whisk cake mix with soda until smooth.

Evenly distribute cake batter among the lined cups of the muffin pan, and smooth out with the back of a spoon.

Evenly distribute cream cheese mixture among the cups. Sprinkle with chocolate chips.

Bake until a toothpick inserted into the center of a cupcake comes out mostly clean, 22 to 24 minutes.

Let cool completely, about 40 minutes. Enjoy!

MAKES 12 SERVINGS

Cheesecake Cupcake Tips!

When testing for doneness, make sure both layers are cooked through. And remember to refrigerate any leftover cupcakes!

159 calories per serving

PB Cheesecake Chocolate Cupcakes

You'll Need: 12-cup muffin pan, foil baking cups, medium bowl, electric mixer, large bowl, whisk

Prep: 15 minutes   **Cook:** 25 minutes   **Cool:** 40 minutes

1/12th of recipe (1 cupcake): 154 calories, 4g fat, 367mg sodium, 25g carbs, 1g fiber, 13.5g sugars, 6g protein

Ingredients

One 8-ounce tub fat-free cream cheese
½ cup powdered peanut butter
½ cup fat-free liquid egg substitute
⅓ cup Splenda No Calorie
    Sweetener (granulated)
1 drop vanilla extract
1 ¾ cups moist-style devil's food cake mix
¾ cup club soda
¼ cup mini semi-sweet chocolate chips

Sugar Alternative:

173 calories, 29.5g carbs, 19g sugars

Directions

Preheat oven to 350 degrees. Line a 12-cup muffin pan with foil baking cups.

Place cream cheese in a medium bowl. With an electric mixer set to medium speed, beat until smooth. Add powdered peanut butter, egg substitute, Splenda, and vanilla extract. Beat until smooth.

In a large bowl, whisk cake mix with soda until smooth.

For a pic of this recipe, see the first photo insert. Yay!

Evenly distribute cake batter among the lined cups of the muffin pan, and smooth out with the back of a spoon.

Evenly distribute cream cheese mixture among the cups. Sprinkle with chocolate chips.

Bake until a toothpick inserted into the center of a cupcake comes out mostly clean, 20 to 22 minutes.

Let cool completely, about 40 minutes. Eat up!

MAKES 12 SERVINGS

154
calories per serving

Hungry for More?

See page 8 for the powdered PB 411. And don't miss these other recipes featuring powdered PB: **PB & Chocolate Chilly Whoopie Pie** (page 191) and **Freezy PB S'mores Sandwich** (page 200)!

PB&J Cupcakes

You'll Need: 12-cup muffin pan, foil baking cups or nonstick spray, small nonstick pot, medium bowl, large bowl, whisk

Prep: 20 minutes **Cook:** 35 minutes **Cool:** 30 minutes

1/12th of recipe (1 cupcake): 157 calories, 5g fat, 263mg sodium, 24.5g carbs, 1g fiber, 12.5g sugars, 4g protein

Ingredients

1 tablespoon cornstarch
1 cup frozen unsweetened strawberries, partially thawed and sliced
1 tablespoon granulated white sugar
⅛ teaspoon cinnamon
Dash salt
1¾ cups moist-style white cake mix
½ cup fat-free liquid egg substitute
⅓ cup reduced-fat creamy peanut butter
¾ teaspoon baking powder
2 tablespoons peanut butter baking chips, chopped

No-Calorie Sweetener Alternative:

153 calories, 23.5g carbs, 11.5g sugars

Directions

Preheat oven to 350 degrees. Line a 12-cup muffin pan with foil baking cups, or spray it with nonstick spray.

In a small nonstick pot, combine cornstarch with ¼ cup cold water, and stir to dissolve. Add strawberries, sugar, cinnamon, and salt, and stir well.

Set heat to medium. Stirring frequently, cook until thick and gooey, 12 to 14 minutes.

Transfer to a medium bowl.

In a large bowl, combine cake mix, egg substitute, peanut butter, and baking powder. Add 1 cup water, and whisk until smooth.

Evenly distribute batter among the cups of the muffin pan.

Bake until a toothpick inserted into the center of a cupcake comes out clean, 16 to 18 minutes.

Let cool completely, about 10 minutes in the pan and 20 minutes out of the pan.

Evenly distribute strawberry mixture among the cupcakes, and sprinkle with chopped peanut butter chips. Devour!

MAKES 12 SERVINGS

157 calories per serving

Hungry for More?

For more PB&J, don't miss the **PB&J Cake Pops** (page 88), **Mini PB&J Cheesecakes** (page 116), **PB&J Softies** (page 172), **Smothered PB&J Squares** (page 218), and **PB&J Crunchettes** (page 248). And turn to page 361 for ALL the peanut butter desserts!

Tie-Dye-For Cupcakes

You'll Need: 12-cup muffin pan, foil baking cups or nonstick spray, 4 medium bowls, large bowl, whisk

Prep: 20 minutes   **Cook:** 20 minutes   **Cool:** 25 minutes

1/12th of recipe (1 cupcake): 135 calories, 3g fat, 231mg sodium, 25g carbs, <0.5g fiber, 15g sugars, 1.5g protein

Ingredients

⅓ cup vanilla frosting
1 sugar-free vanilla pudding snack with 60 calories or less
1¾ cups moist-style white cake mix
½ cup fat-free liquid egg substitute
¾ teaspoon baking powder
2 tablespoons rainbow sprinkles
5 drops red food coloring
5 drops blue food coloring
5 drops yellow food coloring

Directions

Preheat oven to 350 degrees. Line a 12-cup muffin pan with foil baking cups, or spray it with nonstick spray.

In a medium bowl, mix frosting with pudding until smooth and uniform. Cover and refrigerate.

In a large bowl, combine cake mix, egg substitute, and baking powder. Add ¾ cup water, and whisk until smooth.

For a pic of this recipe, see the first photo insert. Yay!

Stir in 1 tablespoon sprinkles. Evenly distribute batter among
3 medium bowls.

Mix a different food coloring into the batter in each bowl until uniform.

Evenly distribute red batter among the cups of the muffin pan. Repeat with
blue batter, followed by yellow batter, so that each cup has three layers.

Bake until a toothpick inserted into the center of a cupcake comes out
clean, 16 to 18 minutes.

Let cupcakes cool completely, about 10 minutes in the pan and 15 minutes
out of the pan.

Spread cupcakes with frosting mixture, and sprinkle with remaining
1 tablespoon sprinkles. Enjoy!

MAKES 12 SERVINGS

135 calories per serving

Pumpkin Pie Cupcakes

You'll Need: 12-cup muffin pan, foil baking cups or nonstick spray, medium bowl, large bowl

Prep: 20 minutes   **Cook:** 20 minutes   **Cool:** 35 minutes

1/12ᵗʰ of recipe (1 cupcake): 110 calories, 1.5g fat, 253mg sodium, 22g carbs, 0.5g fiber, 12g sugars, 2.5g protein

Ingredients

¼ cup plus 2 tablespoons fat-free cream cheese
2 tablespoons granulated white sugar
⅛ teaspoon plus ¼ teaspoon cinnamon
½ cup Cool Whip Free (thawed)
1¾ cups moist-style spice cake mix
1 cup canned pure pumpkin
⅓ cup fat-free liquid egg substitute
½ teaspoon baking powder
⅛ teaspoon salt

No-Calorie Sweetener Alternative:

103 calories, 20g carbs, 10g sugars

Directions

Preheat oven to 350 degrees. Line a 12-cup muffin pan with foil baking cups, or spray it with nonstick spray.

In a medium bowl, combine cream cheese, sugar, and ⅛ teaspoon cinnamon. Stir until smooth. Add Cool Whip, and stir until uniform. Cover and refrigerate.

In a large bowl, combine cake mix, pumpkin, egg substitute, baking powder, salt, and remaining ¼ teaspoon cinnamon. Mix until uniform and mostly smooth.

For a pic of this recipe, see the first photo insert. Yay!

Evenly distribute batter among the cups of the muffin pan.

Bake until a toothpick inserted into the center of a cupcake comes out clean, 16 to 18 minutes.

Let cool completely, about 10 minutes in the pan and 25 minutes out of the pan.

Spread cupcakes with cream cheese mixture. Dig in!

MAKES 12 SERVINGS

Canned Pure Pumpkin Alert!

Beware of pure pumpkin's doppelganger, canned pumpkin pie filling. They may look similar, but the pie filling has more than twice as many calories and over three times as much sugar as the pure stuff! Make sure the can you grab only contains pumpkin—no added ingredients.

Apple Streusel Cupcakes

You'll Need: 12-cup muffin pan, foil baking cups or nonstick spray, 2 medium bowls, large bowl, whisk

Prep: 25 minutes   **Cook:** 20 minutes   **Cool:** 35 minutes

1/12th of recipe (1 cupcake): 148 calories, 2.5g fat, 283mg sodium, 28g carbs, 0.5g fiber, 16g sugars, 3g protein

Ingredients

Icing
¼ cup plus 2 tablespoons fat-free cream cheese
2 tablespoons granulated white sugar
½ cup Cool Whip Free (thawed)

Streusel
3 tablespoons whole-wheat flour
3 tablespoons old-fashioned oats
2 tablespoons brown sugar (not packed)
1½ tablespoons light whipped butter or light buttery spread
1 tablespoon granulated white sugar
½ teaspoon cinnamon

Cupcakes
1¾ cups moist-style yellow cake mix
½ cup fat-free liquid egg substitute
1½ teaspoons cinnamon
¾ teaspoon baking powder
½ teaspoon vanilla extract
1 cup peeled and diced Fuji apple

No-Calorie Sweetener Alternative:

138 calories, 25.5g carbs, 13g sugars

For a pic of this recipe, see the first photo insert. Yay!

Directions

Preheat oven to 350 degrees. Line a 12-cup muffin pan with foil baking cups, or spray it with nonstick spray.

To make the icing, in a medium bowl, stir cream cheese with white sugar until smooth. Add Cool Whip, and stir until uniform. Cover and refrigerate.

In another medium bowl, combine all streusel ingredients. Mash and stir until well mixed and crumbly.

In a large bowl, combine all cupcake ingredients *except* apple. Add ¾ cup water, and whisk until smooth.

Stir in apple. Evenly distribute batter among the cups of the muffin pan.

Sprinkle with streusel mixture. Bake until a toothpick inserted into the center of a cupcake comes out clean, 16 to 18 minutes.

Let cool completely, about 10 minutes in the pan and 25 minutes out of the pan.

Top cupcakes with icing, and enjoy!

MAKES 12 SERVINGS

Fuji 411!

We specify Fujis in many apple recipes because Fujis are the BEST. They're the perfect blend of crisp, sweet, and tart. If you can't find Fujis, go for any sweet apple, like Honeycrisp, Pink Lady, or Gala.

148 calories per serving

Caramel Apple Cupcakes

You'll Need: 12-cup muffin pan, foil baking cups or nonstick spray, medium-large bowl, large bowl, whisk

Prep: 25 minutes   **Cook:** 20 minutes   **Cool:** 40 minutes

1/12th of recipe (1 cupcake): 127 calories, 2.5g fat, 243mg sodium, 25g carbs, 0.5g fiber, 14g sugars, 2g protein

Ingredients

2 cups peeled and diced apples
1 teaspoon cinnamon
1 ¾ cups moist-style yellow cake mix
½ cup fat-free liquid egg substitute
¾ teaspoon baking powder
½ teaspoon vanilla extract
3 tablespoons fat-free, low-fat, or light caramel dip
2 tablespoons chopped peanuts

Directions

Preheat oven to 350 degrees. Line a 12-cup muffin pan with foil baking cups, or spray it with nonstick spray.

In a medium-large bowl, sprinkle apples with ½ teaspoon cinnamon, and toss to coat.

In a large bowl, combine cake mix, egg substitute, baking powder, vanilla extract, and remaining ½ teaspoon cinnamon. Add ¾ cup water, and whisk until smooth.

Stir in cinnamon-coated apples. Evenly distribute mixture among cups of the muffin pan.

Bake until a toothpick inserted into the center of a cupcake comes out clean, 16 to 18 minutes.

Let cool completely, about 10 minutes in the pan and 30 minutes out of the pan.

Spread cupcakes with caramel dip, and sprinkle with peanuts. Mmmm!

MAKES 12 SERVINGS

127 calories per serving

For more recipes, tips & tricks, sign up for FREE daily emails at **hungry-girl.com!**

Banana Split Cuppycakes

You'll Need: 12-cup muffin pan, foil baking cups or nonstick spray, medium bowl, large bowl, whisk

Prep: 15 minutes   **Cook:** 20 minutes   **Cool:** 30 minutes

1/12th of recipe (1 cupcake): 147 calories, 3g fat, 204mg sodium, 28.5g carbs, 0.5g fiber, 16.5g sugars, 1.5g protein

Ingredients

2 tablespoons low-sugar strawberry preserves
1 cup Cool Whip Free (thawed)
1 ¾ cups moist-style yellow cake mix
⅓ cup fat-free liquid egg substitute
½ teaspoon baking powder
¾ cup mashed ripe banana
¼ cup mini semi-sweet chocolate chips
6 maraschino cherries, halved

Directions

Preheat oven to 350 degrees. Line a 12-cup muffin pan with foil baking cups, or spray it with nonstick spray.

In a medium bowl, fold preserves into Cool Whip. Cover and refrigerate.

In a large bowl, combine cake mix, egg substitute, and baking powder. Add 1 cup water, and whisk until smooth.

Stir in banana and 3 tablespoons chocolate chips. Evenly distribute batter among the cups of the muffin pan.

Bake until a toothpick inserted into the center of a cupcake comes out clean, 18 to 20 minutes.

Let cool completely, about 10 minutes in the pan and 20 minutes out of the pan.

Spread cupcakes with Cool Whip mixture, and sprinkle with remaining 1 tablespoon chocolate chips. Top each cupcake with a cherry half, and enjoy!

MAKES 12 SERVINGS

147 calories per serving

Strawberry
Snowball Cupcakes

You'll Need: 12-cup muffin pan, foil baking cups or nonstick spray, small blender or food processor, large bowl, whisk

Prep: 10 minutes   **Cook:** 20 minutes   **Cool:** 25 minutes

1/12th of recipe (1 cupcake): 135 calories, 3.5g fat, 226mg sodium, 24.5g carbs, 1g fiber, 13g sugars, 2g protein

Ingredients

1½ cups frozen unsweetened strawberries, thawed (not drained)
1¾ cups moist-style white cake mix
½ cup fat-free liquid egg substitute
¾ teaspoon baking powder
1 drop red food coloring
1½ cups Cool Whip Free (thawed)
½ cup shredded sweetened coconut

Directions

Preheat oven to 350 degrees. Line a 12-cup muffin pan with foil baking cups, or spray it with nonstick spray.

Place thawed strawberries (and any excess liquid) in a small blender or food processor, and puree until smooth.

Measure out ½ cup pureed strawberries, and transfer to a large bowl. (Discard any excess puree, or save for another use.)

Add cake mix, egg substitute, baking powder, and food coloring to the large bowl. Add ½ cup water, and whisk until smooth.

Evenly distribute batter among the cups of the muffin pan.

Bake until a toothpick inserted into the center of a cupcake comes out clean, 16 to 18 minutes.

Let cool completely, about 10 minutes in the pan and 15 minutes out of the pan.

Spread cupcakes with Cool Whip, sprinkle with coconut, and devour!

MAKES 12 SERVINGS

135 calories per serving

Very Vanilla Fluffcakes

You'll Need: 12-cup muffin pan, foil baking cups or nonstick spray, medium bowl, large bowl, whisk, metal or glass bowl, electric mixer

Prep: 15 minutes   **Cook:** 20 minutes   **Cool:** 25 minutes

1/12th of recipe (1 cupcake): 146 calories, 3.5g fat, 252mg sodium, 26.5g carbs, <0.5g fiber, 16.5g sugars, 2g protein

Ingredients

⅓ cup vanilla frosting
1 sugar-free vanilla pudding snack with 60 calories or less
1¾ cups moist-style yellow cake mix
¾ teaspoon baking powder
½ teaspoon vanilla extract
1 cup club soda
½ cup liquid egg whites (about 4 egg whites)
3 tablespoons rainbow sprinkles

Directions

Preheat oven to 350 degrees. Line a 12-cup muffin pan with foil baking cups, or spray it with nonstick spray.

In a medium bowl, mix frosting with pudding until smooth and uniform. Cover and refrigerate.

In a large bowl, combine cake mix, baking powder, and vanilla extract. Add soda, and whisk until smooth.

Place egg whites in a metal or glass bowl. With an electric mixer set to medium speed, beat until fluffy and slightly stiff, 3 to 4 minutes.

Gently fold egg whites into batter until uniform. Evenly distribute batter among the cups of the muffin pan.

Bake until a toothpick inserted into the center of a cupcake comes out mostly clean, 16 to 18 minutes.

Let cool completely, about 10 minutes in the pan and 15 minutes out of the pan.

Spread cupcakes with frosting mixture, and sprinkle with sprinkles!

MAKES 12 SERVINGS

146 calories per serving

Vanilla Latte Cupcakes

You'll Need: 12-cup muffin pan, foil baking cups or nonstick spray, medium bowl, glass, large bowl, whisk

Prep: 15 minutes   **Cook:** 20 minutes   **Cool:** 25 minutes

> **1/12th of recipe (1 cupcake):** 127 calories, 3g fat, 238mg sodium, 23.5g carbs, <0.5g fiber, 13.5g sugars, 2g protein

Ingredients

⅓ cup vanilla frosting
1 sugar-free vanilla pudding snack with 60 calories or less
1 tablespoon plus 1 teaspoon instant coffee granules
1¾ cups moist-style white cake mix
½ cup fat-free liquid egg substitute
¾ teaspoon baking powder

Optional topping: cocoa powder

Directions

Preheat oven to 350 degrees. Line a 12-cup muffin pan with foil baking cups, or spray it with nonstick spray.

In a medium bowl, mix frosting with pudding until smooth and uniform. Cover and refrigerate.

Place coffee granules in a glass. Add ¼ cup hot water, and stir to dissolve. Add ¾ cup cold water.

In a large bowl, combine cake mix, egg substitute, baking powder, and coffee mixture. Whisk until smooth.

Evenly distribute batter among the cups of the muffin pan.

Bake until a toothpick inserted into the center of a cupcake comes out clean, 16 to 18 minutes.

Let cupcakes cool completely, about 10 minutes in the pan and 15 minutes out of the pan.

Spread cupcakes with frosting mixture, and enjoy!

MAKES 12 SERVINGS

127 calories per serving

CHAPTER 3

CAKE POPS

People are obsessed with cake pops. They're cute and FUN to eat—and portion-controlled cake is a no-brainer. We actually went a little crazy with the cake-on-a-stick recipes in this chapter. There are many. And they are DELICIOUS.

CAKE POP TIPS & TRICKS . . .

Stick It! Lollipop sticks are often found in the baking-supplies aisle of supermarkets and stores like Target and Walmart. Craft stores (like Michaels) are also good places to look. If all else fails, buy 'em online!

Batter Up! Many of these recipes feature batters made from cake mix and canned pumpkin. The batter will remain thick and may not become *completely* smooth. Worry not—this is to be expected!

Cool It! For best results, use a cooling rack. No rack? Use a plate!

Roll with It! Dampen your hands before rolling the cake into balls. It moistens the crumbs and helps the cake form together easily.

Fo' Drizzle! If you have melted chocolate left over once all the cake balls are coated, feel free to evenly drizzle the remainder over your treats!

Coconut Patty Cake Pops

You'll Need: 8-inch by 8-inch baking pan, nonstick spray, 2 large bowls, cooling rack, baking sheet, wax/parchment paper, plate, medium microwave-safe bowl, lollipop sticks

Prep: 30 minutes   **Cook:** 25 minutes   **Cool/Chill:** 1 hour and 20 minutes

1/18th of recipe (1 pop): 107 calories, 3.5g fat, 143mg sodium, 18.5g carbs, 1.5g fiber, 11g sugars, 1g protein

Ingredients

1 ¾ cups moist-style devil's food cake mix
1 cup canned pure pumpkin
1 ½ teaspoons coconut extract
⅓ cup shredded sweetened coconut
½ cup mini semi-sweet chocolate chips

Directions

Preheat oven to 400 degrees. Spray an 8-inch by 8-inch baking pan with nonstick spray.

In a large bowl, combine cake mix, pumpkin, and coconut extract. Mix until smooth and uniform. Spread batter into the baking pan.

Bake until a toothpick inserted into the center comes out clean, about 18 minutes.

Let cool completely, about 30 minutes in the pan and 30 minutes out of the pan on a cooling rack.

Line a baking sheet with wax/parchment paper. Clear a space in your fridge for the baking sheet.

Break cake into pieces, and place in a large bowl. Use your hands to crumble cake into very small pieces. Thoroughly knead into a ball.

On a dry surface, form cake into a log of even thickness, about 9 inches long. Cut log into 18 evenly sized pieces, and form each piece into a ball.

Spread out shredded coconut on a plate.

Place chocolate chips in a medium microwave-safe bowl, and microwave at 50 percent power for 1 minute.

Vigorously stir, and microwave at 50 percent power for 30 seconds. Repeat, as needed, until completely melted.

Gently dunk and swirl a cake ball into the melted chocolate, evenly coating the top half. Gently press into the shredded coconut. Place on the wax/parchment paper, coconut side down.

Repeat with remaining cake balls, reheating chocolate at 50 percent power and vigorously stirring, as needed.

Insert a lollipop stick into the top of each ball, stopping at the center.

Refrigerate until chocolate has completely hardened, about 20 minutes. Yum time!

MAKES 18 SERVINGS

107 calories per serving

Minty Chocolate Cake Pops

You'll Need: 8-inch by 8-inch baking pan, nonstick spray, 2 large bowls, cooling rack, baking sheet, wax/parchment paper, medium microwave-safe bowl, lollipop sticks

Prep: 30 minutes   **Cook:** 25 minutes   **Cool/Chill:** 1 hour and 20 minutes

1/18th of recipe (1 pop): 96 calories, 3g fat, 136mg sodium, 17g carbs, 1g fiber, 10.5g sugars, 1g protein

Ingredients

1¾ cups moist-style devil's food cake mix
1 cup canned pure pumpkin
¼ teaspoon peppermint extract
½ cup mini semi-sweet chocolate chips

Directions

Preheat oven to 400 degrees. Spray an 8-inch by 8-inch baking pan with nonstick spray.

In a large bowl, combine cake mix, pumpkin, and peppermint extract. Mix until smooth and uniform. Spread batter into the baking pan.

Bake until a toothpick inserted into the center comes out clean, about 18 minutes.

Let cool completely, about 30 minutes in the pan and 30 minutes out of the pan on a cooling rack.

Line a baking sheet with wax/parchment paper. Clear a space in your fridge for the baking sheet.

Break cake into pieces, and place in a large bowl. Use your hands to crumble cake into very small pieces. Thoroughly knead into a ball.

On a dry surface, form cake into a log of even thickness, about 9 inches long. Cut log into 18 evenly sized pieces, and form each piece into a ball.

Place chocolate chips in a medium microwave-safe bowl, and microwave at 50 percent power for 1 minute.

Vigorously stir, and microwave at 50 percent power for 30 seconds. Repeat, as needed, until completely melted.

Gently dunk and swirl a cake ball into the melted chocolate, evenly coating the top half. Place on the wax/parchment paper, melted-chocolate side down.

Repeat with remaining cake balls, reheating chocolate at 50 percent power and vigorously stirring, as needed.

Insert a lollipop stick into the top of each ball, stopping at the center.

Refrigerate until chocolate has completely hardened, about 20 minutes. Mmmm!

MAKES 18 SERVINGS

96 calories per serving

* Flip to the photo inserts to see dozens of recipe pics! And for photos of ALL the recipes, go to **hungry-girl.com/books**.

Walnut Brownie Pops

You'll Need: 8-inch by 8-inch baking pan, nonstick spray, 2 large bowls, cooling rack, baking sheet, wax/parchment paper, plate, medium microwave-safe bowl, lollipop sticks

Prep: 30 minutes   **Cook:** 25 minutes   **Cool/Chill:** 1 hour and 20 minutes

1/18th of recipe (1 pop): 110 calories, 4g fat, 136mg sodium, 17.5g carbs, 1g fiber, 10.5g sugars, 1.5g protein

Ingredients

1¾ cups moist-style devil's food cake mix
1 cup canned pure pumpkin
⅓ cup very finely chopped walnuts
½ cup mini semi-sweet chocolate chips

Directions

Preheat oven to 400 degrees. Spray an 8-inch by 8-inch baking pan with nonstick spray.

In a large bowl, mix cake mix with pumpkin until smooth and uniform. Spread batter into the baking pan.

Bake until a toothpick inserted into the center comes out clean, about 18 minutes.

Let cool completely, about 30 minutes in the pan and 30 minutes out of the pan on a cooling rack.

Line a baking sheet with wax/parchment paper. Clear a space in your fridge for the baking sheet.

Break cake into pieces, and place in a large bowl. Use your hands to crumble cake into very small pieces. Thoroughly knead into a ball.

For a pic of this recipe, see the first photo insert. Yay!

On a dry surface, form cake into a log of even thickness, about 9 inches long. Cut log into 18 evenly sized pieces, and form each piece into a ball.

Spread out walnuts on a plate.

Place chocolate chips in a medium microwave-safe bowl, and microwave at 50 percent power for 1 minute.

Vigorously stir, and microwave at 50 percent power for 30 seconds. Repeat, as needed, until completely melted.

Gently dunk and swirl a cake ball into the melted chocolate, evenly coating the top half. Gently press into the walnuts. Place on the wax/parchment paper, walnut side down.

Repeat with remaining cake balls, reheating chocolate at 50 percent power and vigorously stirring, as needed.

Insert a lollipop stick into the top of each ball, stopping at the center.

Refrigerate until chocolate has completely hardened, about 20 minutes. Eat up!

MAKES 18 SERVINGS

110 calories per serving

Black 'n White Cake Pops

You'll Need: 8-inch by 8-inch baking pan, nonstick spray, 2 large bowls, cooling rack, baking sheet, wax/parchment paper, medium microwave-safe bowl, lollipop sticks

Prep: 30 minutes   **Cook:** 25 minutes   **Cool:** 1 hour and 10 minutes

1/18th of recipe (1 pop): 99 calories, 3g fat, 142mg sodium, 17.5g carbs, 1g fiber, 11g sugars, 1g protein

Ingredients

1¾ cups moist-style devil's food cake mix
1 cup canned pure pumpkin
½ cup white chocolate chips

Directions

Preheat oven to 400 degrees. Spray an 8-inch by 8-inch baking pan with nonstick spray.

In a large bowl, mix cake mix with pumpkin until smooth and uniform. Spread batter into the baking pan.

Bake until a toothpick inserted into the center comes out clean, about 18 minutes.

Let cool completely, about 30 minutes in the pan and 30 minutes out of the pan on a cooling rack.

Line a baking sheet with wax/parchment paper.

Break cake into pieces, and place in a large bowl. Use your hands to crumble cake into very small pieces. Thoroughly knead into a ball.

On a dry surface, form cake into a log of even thickness, about 9 inches long. Cut log into 18 evenly sized pieces, and form each piece into a ball.

Place white chocolate chips in a medium microwave-safe bowl, and microwave at 50 percent power for 1 minute.

Vigorously stir, and microwave at 50 percent power for 30 seconds. Repeat, as needed, until completely melted.

Gently dunk and swirl a cake ball into the melted white chocolate, evenly coating the top half. Place on the wax/parchment paper, white chocolate side down.

Repeat with remaining cake balls, reheating white chocolate at 50 percent power and vigorously stirring, as needed.

Insert a lollipop stick into the top of each ball, stopping at the center.

Let cool until white chocolate has completely hardened, about 10 minutes. Mmmm!

MAKES 18 SERVINGS

99 calories per serving

For more recipes, tips & tricks, sign up for FREE daily emails at **hungry-girl.com!**

Roarin' Red Velvet Cake Pops

You'll Need: 8-inch by 8-inch baking pan, nonstick spray, 2 large bowls, whisk, cooling rack, baking sheet, wax/parchment paper, medium microwave-safe bowl, lollipop sticks

Prep: 30 minutes   **Cook:** 30 minutes   **Cool:** 1 hour and 10 minutes

1/18th of recipe (1 pop): 93 calories, 3g fat, 87mg sodium, 15g carbs, 0.5g fiber, 10g sugars, 1g protein

Ingredients

1 ¾ cups Duncan Hines Signature Red Velvet Cake Mix
1 cup canned pure pumpkin
½ cup white chocolate chips

Directions

Preheat oven to 375 degrees. Spray an 8-inch by 8-inch baking pan with nonstick spray.

In a large bowl, whisk cake mix until mostly free of lumps. Add pumpkin, and mix until completely smooth and uniform. Spread batter into the baking pan.

Bake until a toothpick inserted into the center comes out clean, about 26 minutes.

Let cool completely, about 30 minutes in the pan and 30 minutes out of the pan on a cooling rack.

Line a baking sheet with wax/parchment paper.

Break cake into pieces, and place in a large bowl. Use your hands to crumble cake into very small pieces. Thoroughly knead into a ball.

On a dry surface, form cake into a log of even thickness, about 9 inches long. Cut log into 18 evenly sized pieces, and form each piece into a ball.

Place white chocolate chips in a medium microwave-safe bowl, and microwave at 50 percent power for 1 minute.

Vigorously stir, and microwave at 50 percent power for 30 seconds. Repeat, as needed, until completely melted.

Gently dunk and swirl a cake ball into the melted white chocolate, evenly coating the top half. Place on the wax/parchment paper, white chocolate side down.

Repeat with remaining cake balls, reheating white chocolate at 50 percent power and vigorously stirring, as needed.

Insert a lollipop stick into the top of each ball, stopping at the center.

Let cool until white chocolate has completely hardened, about 10 minutes. Enjoy!

MAKES 18 SERVINGS

Happy Holidays Spice Cake Pops

You'll Need: 8-inch by 8-inch baking pan, nonstick spray, 2 large bowls, cooling rack, baking sheet, wax/parchment paper, plate, medium microwave-safe bowl, lollipop sticks

Prep: 30 minutes   **Cook:** 25 minutes   **Cool:** 1 hour and 10 minutes

1/18ᵗʰ of recipe (1 pop): 104 calories, 4g fat, 100mg sodium, 16.5g carbs, 0.5g fiber, 10g sugars, 1g protein

Ingredients

1¾ cups moist-style spice cake mix
1 cup canned pure pumpkin
⅓ cup very finely chopped walnuts
½ cup white chocolate chips
⅛ teaspoon cinnamon

Directions

Preheat oven to 400 degrees. Spray an 8-inch by 8-inch baking pan with nonstick spray.

In a large bowl, mix cake mix with pumpkin until smooth and uniform. Spread batter into the baking pan.

Bake until a toothpick inserted into the center comes out clean, about 18 minutes.

Let cool completely, about 30 minutes in the pan and 30 minutes out of the pan on a cooling rack.

Line a baking sheet with wax/parchment paper.

Break cake into pieces, and place in a large bowl. Use your hands to crumble cake into very small pieces. Thoroughly knead into a ball.

On a dry surface, form cake into a log of even thickness, about 9 inches long. Cut log into 18 evenly sized pieces, and form each piece into a ball.

Spread out walnuts on a plate.

Place white chocolate chips in a medium microwave-safe bowl, and microwave at 50 percent power for 1 minute.

Vigorously stir, and microwave at 50 percent power for 30 seconds. Repeat, as needed, until completely melted.

Stir cinnamon into the melted white chocolate. Gently dunk and swirl a cake ball into the melted chocolate, evenly coating the top half. Gently press into walnuts. Place on the wax/parchment paper, walnut side down.

Repeat with remaining cake balls, reheating white chocolate at 50 percent power and vigorously stirring, as needed.

Insert a lollipop stick into the top of each ball, stopping at the center.

Let cool until white chocolate has completely hardened, about 10 minutes. Eat up!

MAKES 18 SERVINGS

Candy Cane Cake Pops

You'll Need: 8-inch by 8-inch baking pan, nonstick spray, 2 large bowls, cooling rack, baking sheet, wax/parchment paper, plate, medium microwave-safe bowl, lollipop sticks

Prep: 30 minutes   **Cook:** 25 minutes   **Cool:** 1 hour and 10 minutes

1/18th of recipe (1 pop): 106 calories, 3g fat, 142mg sodium, 19g carbs, 1g fiber, 12.5g sugars, 1g protein

Ingredients

1 ¾ cups moist-style devil's food cake mix
1 cup canned pure pumpkin
⅛ teaspoon peppermint extract
2 standard-sized candy canes or 8 mini candy canes, crushed
½ cup white chocolate chips

Directions

Preheat oven to 400 degrees. Spray an 8-inch by 8-inch baking pan with nonstick spray.

In a large bowl, combine cake mix, pumpkin, and peppermint extract. Mix until smooth and uniform. Spread batter into the baking pan.

Bake until a toothpick inserted into the center comes out clean, about 18 minutes.

Let cool completely, about 30 minutes in the pan and 30 minutes out of the pan on a cooling rack.

Line a baking sheet with wax/parchment paper.

Break cake into pieces, and place in a large bowl. Use your hands to crumble cake into very small pieces. Thoroughly knead into a ball.

On a dry surface, form cake into a log of even thickness, about 9 inches long. Cut log into 18 evenly sized pieces, and form each piece into a ball.

Spread out crushed candy canes on a plate.

Place white chocolate chips in a medium microwave-safe bowl, and microwave at 50 percent power for 1 minute.

Vigorously stir, and microwave at 50 percent power for 30 seconds. Repeat, as needed, until completely melted.

Gently dunk and swirl a cake ball into the melted white chocolate, evenly coating the top half. Gently press into the crushed candy canes. Place back on wax/parchment paper, white chocolate side down.

Repeat with remaining cake balls, reheating white chocolate at 50 percent power and vigorously stirring, as needed.

Insert a lollipop stick into the top of each ball, stopping at the center.

Let cool until white chocolate has completely hardened, about 10 minutes. Yay!

MAKES 18 SERVINGS

106 calories per serving

Hungry for More?

For more candy-cane concoctions, see the **Chocolate Chip Candy Cane Cheesecake** (page 112) and **Candy Cane Brownies** (page 126)!

Creamsicle Cake Pops

You'll Need: 8-inch by 8-inch baking pan, nonstick spray, 2 large bowls, cooling rack, baking sheet, wax/parchment paper, plate, medium microwave-safe bowl, lollipop sticks

Prep: 30 minutes   **Cook:** 25 minutes   **Cool:** 1 hour and 10 minutes

1/18th of recipe (1 pop): 96 calories, 2.5g fat, 111mg sodium, 17g carbs, 0.5g fiber, 10.5g sugars, 1g protein

Ingredients

1¾ cups moist-style white cake mix
1 cup canned pure pumpkin
¼ teaspoon orange extract
½ cup white chocolate chips

Directions

Preheat oven to 400 degrees. Spray an 8-inch by 8-inch baking pan with nonstick spray.

In a large bowl, combine cake mix, pumpkin, and orange extract. Mix until completely smooth and uniform. Spread batter into the baking pan.

Bake until a toothpick inserted into the center comes out clean, about 18 minutes.

Let cool completely, about 30 minutes in the pan and 30 minutes out of the pan on a cooling rack.

Line a baking sheet with wax/parchment paper.

Break cake into pieces, and place in a large bowl. Use your hands to crumble cake into very small pieces. Thoroughly knead into a ball.

On a dry surface, form cake into a log of even thickness, about 9 inches long. Cut log into 18 evenly sized pieces, and form each piece into a ball.

Place white chocolate chips in a medium microwave-safe bowl, and microwave at 50 percent power for 1 minute.

Vigorously stir, and microwave at 50 percent power for 30 seconds. Repeat, as needed, until completely melted.

Gently dunk and swirl a cake ball into the melted white chocolate, evenly coating the top half. Place on the wax/parchment paper, white chocolate side down.

Repeat with remaining cake balls, reheating white chocolate at 50 percent power and vigorously stirring, as needed.

Insert a lollipop stick into the top of each ball, stopping at the center.

Let cool until white chocolate has completely hardened, about 10 minutes. Enjoy!

MAKES 18 SERVINGS

96 calories per serving

Birthday Cake Pops

You'll Need: 8-inch by 8-inch baking pan, nonstick spray, 2 large bowls, cooling rack, baking sheet, wax/parchment paper, plate, medium microwave-safe bowl, lollipop sticks

Prep: 30 minutes   **Cook:** 25 minutes   **Cool:** 1 hour and 10 minutes

1/18th of recipe (1 pop): 90 calories, 3g fat, 119mg sodium, 15.5g carbs, <0.5g fiber, 10g sugars, 0.5g protein

Ingredients

1¾ cups Funfetti or rainbow chip moist-style cake mix
¾ cup club soda
1½ tablespoons rainbow sprinkles
½ cup white chocolate chips

Directions

Preheat oven to 375 degrees. Spray an 8-inch by 8-inch baking pan with nonstick spray.

In a large bowl, mix cake mix with club soda until smooth and uniform. Spread batter into the baking pan.

Bake until a toothpick inserted into the center comes out clean, about 20 minutes.

Let cool completely, about 30 minutes in the pan and 30 minutes out of the pan on a cooling rack.

Line a baking sheet with wax/parchment paper.

Break cake into pieces, and place in a large bowl. Use your hands to crumble cake into very small pieces. Thoroughly knead into a ball.

For a pic of this recipe, see the first photo insert. Yay!

On a dry surface, form cake into a log of even thickness, about 9 inches long. Cut log into 18 evenly sized pieces, and form each piece into a ball.

Spread out sprinkles on a plate.

Place white chocolate chips in a medium microwave-safe bowl, and microwave at 50 percent power for 1 minute.

Vigorously stir, and microwave at 50 percent power for 30 seconds. Repeat, as needed, until completely melted.

Gently dunk and swirl a cake ball into the melted white chocolate, evenly coating the top half. Gently press into sprinkles. Place on the wax/parchment paper, white chocolate side down.

Repeat with remaining cake balls, reheating white chocolate at 50 percent power and vigorously stirring, as needed.

Insert a lollipop stick into the top of each ball, stopping at the center.

Let cool until white chocolate has completely hardened, about 10 minutes. Yum!

MAKES 18 SERVINGS

90 calories per serving

Chocolate PB Cake Pops

You'll Need: 8-inch by 8-inch baking pan, nonstick spray, 2 large bowls, cooling rack, baking sheet, wax/parchment paper, medium microwave-safe bowl, lollipop sticks

Prep: 30 minutes   **Cook:** 25 minutes   **Cool:** 1 hour and 5 minutes

1/18th of recipe (1 pop): 101 calories, 3g fat, 153mg sodium, 16.5g carbs, 1g fiber, 9.5g sugars, 1.5g protein

Ingredients

1 ¾ cups moist-style devil's food cake mix
1 cup canned pure pumpkin
½ cup peanut butter baking chips

Directions

Preheat oven to 400 degrees. Spray an 8-inch by 8-inch baking pan with nonstick spray.

In a large bowl, mix cake mix with pumpkin until smooth and uniform. Spread batter into the baking pan.

Bake until a toothpick inserted into the center comes out clean, about 18 minutes.

Let cool completely, about 30 minutes in the pan and 30 minutes out of the pan on a cooling rack.

Line a baking sheet with wax/parchment paper.

Break cake into pieces, and place in a large bowl. Use your hands to crumble cake into very small pieces. Thoroughly knead into a ball.

For a pic of this recipe, see the first photo insert. Yay!

On a dry surface, form cake into a log of even thickness, about 9 inches long. Cut log into 18 evenly sized pieces, and form each piece into a ball.

Place peanut butter chips in a medium microwave-safe bowl, and microwave at 50 percent power for 1 minute.

Vigorously stir, and microwave at 50 percent power for 30 seconds. Repeat, as needed, until completely melted.

Spoon and spread melted peanut butter onto a cake ball, evenly coating the top half. Place on the wax/parchment paper, peanut butter side down.

Repeat with remaining cake balls, reheating peanut butter chips at 50 percent power and stirring, if needed.

Insert a lollipop stick into the top of each ball, stopping at the center.

Let cool until peanut butter has completely hardened, about 5 minutes. Eat up!

MAKES 18 SERVINGS

PB&J Cake Pops

You'll Need: 8-inch by 8-inch baking pan, nonstick spray, 2 large bowls, cooling rack, baking sheet, wax/parchment paper, medium microwave-safe bowl, lollipop sticks

Prep: 30 minutes   **Cook:** 25 minutes   **Cool:** 1 hour and 5 minutes

1/18th of recipe (1 pop): 93 calories, 3g fat, 135mg sodium, 15g carbs, <0.5g fiber, 9g sugars, 1g protein

Ingredients

1 ¾ cups moist-style strawberry cake mix
¾ cup club soda
½ cup peanut butter baking chips

Directions

Preheat oven to 375 degrees. Spray an 8-inch by 8-inch baking pan with nonstick spray.

In a large bowl, mix cake mix with club soda until completely smooth and uniform. Spread batter into the baking pan.

Bake until a toothpick inserted into the center comes out clean, about 20 minutes.

Let cool completely, about 30 minutes in the pan and 30 minutes out of the pan on a cooling rack.

Line a baking sheet with wax/parchment paper.

Break cake into pieces, and place in a large bowl. Use your hands to crumble cake into very small pieces. Thoroughly knead into a ball.

On a dry surface, form cake into a log of even thickness, about 9 inches long.

Cut log into 18 evenly sized pieces, and form each piece into a ball.

Place peanut butter chips in a medium microwave-safe bowl, and microwave at 50 percent power for 1 minute.

Vigorously stir, and microwave at 50 percent power for 30 seconds. Repeat, as needed, until completely melted.

Spoon and spread melted peanut butter onto a cake ball, evenly coating the top half. Place on the wax/parchment paper, peanut butter side down.

Repeat with remaining cake balls, reheating peanut butter at 50 percent power and stirring, if needed.

Insert a lollipop stick into the top of each ball, stopping at the center.

Let cool until peanut butter has completely hardened, about 5 minutes. Cake pop time!

MAKES 18 SERVINGS

CHAPTER 4

CAKES & CHEESECAKES

From red velvet to cookies 'n cream, every cake you could possibly desire is right here in this chapter. Try not to drool on the pages . . .

CAKES

Cake is wonderful—it just is. And there's absolutely no reason this book shouldn't have LOTS of super-easy cake recipes. So, um, here they are!

NEED-TO-KNOW CAKE INFO . . .

It's important to use a cooling rack with these recipes. Otherwise, you'll wind up with soggy-bottomed cakes. *Nobody* likes a soggy bottom . . .

2-Ingredient
Pineapple Bliss Cake

You'll Need: 9-inch round cake pan, nonstick spray, large bowl, cooling rack, plate

Prep: 5 minutes   **Cook:** 20 minutes   **Cool:** 1 hour

¹⁄₈ᵗʰ of cake: 150 calories, 2.5g fat, 253mg sodium, 31g carbs, <0.5g fiber, 18g sugars, 1g protein

Ingredients

1 ¾ cups moist-style yellow cake mix
One 8-ounce can crushed pineapple in juice (not drained)

Directions

Preheat oven to 350 degrees. Spray a 9-inch round cake pan with nonstick spray.

In a large bowl, stir cake mix with undrained pineapple until uniform. (Batter will be thick!)

Spread batter into the cake pan.

Bake until a toothpick inserted into the center comes out mostly clean, 18 to 20 minutes.

Let cool completely, about 30 minutes in the pan and 30 minutes out of the pan on a cooling rack.

Plate cake, and serve!

MAKES 8 SERVINGS

HG Tip!

This cake is super moist and crumbly. Slice it with a damp knife to keep it from falling apart. (It's delicious, no matter what!)

150 calories per serving

Maple Cream Pumpkin 'n Spice Cake

You'll Need: 9-inch round cake pan, nonstick spray, medium bowl, large bowl, whisk, cooling rack, plate

Prep: 15 minutes   **Cook:** 20 minutes   **Cool:** 1 hour

1/8th of cake: 162 calories, 2.5g fat, 386mg sodium, 32g carbs, 0.5g fiber, 16g sugars, 2.5g protein

Ingredients

¼ cup plus 2 tablespoons fat-free cream cheese
2 no-calorie sweetener packets
⅛ teaspoon plus ½ teaspoon cinnamon
½ cup Cool Whip Free (thawed)
2 tablespoons sugar-free pancake syrup
¼ teaspoon maple extract
1 ¾ cups moist-style yellow cake mix
½ cup canned pure pumpkin
¾ teaspoon baking powder
½ teaspoon pumpkin pie spice

Directions

Preheat oven to 350 degrees. Spray a 9-inch round cake pan with nonstick spray.

In a medium bowl, combine cream cheese with sweetener. Add ⅛ teaspoon cinnamon, and stir until smooth. Add Cool Whip, syrup, and maple extract, and stir until uniform. Cover and refrigerate.

In a large bowl, combine cake mix, pumpkin, baking powder, and pumpkin pie spice. Add ½ cup water and remaining ½ teaspoon cinnamon.

Whisk until smooth. Spread batter into the cake pan.

Bake until a toothpick inserted into the center comes out clean, 16 to 18 minutes.

Let cool completely, about 30 minutes in the pan and 30 minutes out of the pan on a cooling rack.

Plate cake, and spread with cream cheese mixture. Dig in!

MAKES 8 SERVINGS

162 calories per serving

✳ Flip to the photo inserts to see dozens of recipe pics! And for photos of ALL the recipes, go to **hungry-girl.com/books.**

24-Carat Cake

You'll Need: 9-inch round cake pan, nonstick spray, medium bowl, large bowl, whisk, cooling rack, plate

Prep: 25 minutes   **Cook:** 30 minutes   **Cool:** 1½ hours

1/10th of cake: 193 calories, 4g fat, 313mg sodium, 34.5g carbs, 3g fiber, 15.5g sugars, 5.5g protein

Ingredients

Frosting
4 ounces (about ½ cup) fat-free cream cheese
2 tablespoons Splenda No Calorie Sweetener (granulated)
½ cup Cool Whip Free (thawed)

Cake
1 cup moist-style yellow cake mix
¾ cup whole-wheat flour
¾ cup canned pure pumpkin
⅔ cup fat-free liquid egg substitute
½ cup Splenda No Calorie Sweetener (granulated)
2 tablespoons brown sugar (not packed)
1½ teaspoons pumpkin pie spice
1½ teaspoons cinnamon
1 teaspoon baking powder
1½ cups bagged shredded carrots, roughly chopped
⅔ cup crushed pineapple packed in juice (not drained)

Toppings
2 tablespoons fat-free, low-fat, or light caramel dip
3 tablespoons shredded sweetened coconut
3 tablespoons chopped pecans

Directions

Preheat oven to 350 degrees. Spray a 9-inch round cake pan with nonstick spray.

To make the frosting, in a medium bowl, thoroughly mix cream cheese with Splenda. Add Cool Whip, and stir until uniform. Cover and refrigerate.

In a large bowl, combine all cake ingredients *except* carrots and pineapple. Add ¼ cup water, and whisk until smooth and uniform.

Stir in carrots and undrained pineapple. Pour batter into the cake pan, and smooth out the top.

Bake until a toothpick inserted into the center comes out clean, 28 to 30 minutes.

Let cool completely, about 30 minutes in the pan and 1 hour out of the pan on a cooling rack.

Plate cake, and spread with frosting. Drizzle with caramel, and sprinkle with coconut and pecans. Eat up!

MAKES 10 SERVINGS

193 calories per serving

Vanilla Caramel Dream Cake

You'll Need: 9-inch round cake pan, nonstick spray, medium bowl, large bowl, whisk, cooling rack, plate

Prep: 15 minutes   **Cook:** 30 minutes   **Cool:** 1 hour

1/10th of cake: 167 calories, 3.5g fat, 300mg sodium, 32.5g carbs, <0.5g fiber, 19.5g sugars, 1.5g protein

Ingredients

⅓ cup vanilla frosting
1 sugar-free vanilla pudding snack with 60 calories or less
3 tablespoons fat-free, low-fat, or light caramel dip
1¾ cups moist-style yellow cake mix
½ cup fat-free liquid egg substitute
¾ teaspoon baking powder

Directions

Preheat oven to 350 degrees. Spray a 9-inch round cake pan with nonstick spray.

In a medium bowl, combine frosting with pudding. Add 2 tablespoons caramel dip, and stir until smooth and uniform. Cover and refrigerate.

In a large bowl, combine cake mix, egg substitute, and baking powder. Add 1 cup water, and whisk until smooth.

Pour batter into the cake pan.

For a pic of this recipe, see the first photo insert. Yay!

Bake until a toothpick inserted into the center comes out clean, 24 to 26 minutes.

Let cool completely, about 30 minutes in the pan and 30 minutes out of the pan on a cooling rack.

Plate cake, and spread the top with frosting mixture. Drizzle with remaining 1 tablespoon caramel dip. Dig in!

MAKES 10 SERVINGS

167 calories per serving

For more recipes, tips & tricks, sign up for FREE daily emails at **hungry-girl.com!**

Cookies 'n Cream Cake

You'll Need: 9-inch round cake pan, nonstick spray, medium bowl, large bowl, whisk, cooling rack, plate

Prep: 15 minutes   **Cook:** 30 minutes   **Cool:** 1 hour

1/10th of cake: 177 calories, 4g fat, 363mg sodium, 32.5g carbs, 1g fiber, 18.5g sugars, 3g protein

Ingredients

⅓ cup vanilla frosting
1 sugar-free vanilla pudding snack with 60 calories or less
1 ¾ cups moist-style devil's food cake mix
½ cup fat-free liquid egg substitute
¾ teaspoon baking powder
2 packs Nabisco 100 Cal Oreo Thin Crisps, roughly crushed

HG Alternative: If you can't track down the cookies, use 3 sheets (12 crackers) of chocolate graham crackers instead.

Directions

Preheat oven to 350 degrees. Spray a 9-inch round cake pan with nonstick spray.

In a medium bowl, mix frosting with pudding until smooth and uniform. Cover and refrigerate.

In a large bowl, combine cake mix, egg substitute, and baking powder. Add 1 cup water, and whisk until smooth.

Pour batter into the cake pan.

Bake until a toothpick inserted into the center comes out clean, 24 to 26 minutes.

Let cool completely, about 30 minutes in the pan and 30 minutes out of the pan on a cooling rack.

Plate cake, spread with frosting mixture, and sprinkle with crushed cookies. Eat up!

MAKES 10 SERVINGS

177 calories per serving

Red Velvet Coconut Cream Cake

You'll Need: 9-inch round cake pan, nonstick spray, medium bowl, whisk, glass, large bowl, cooling rack, plate

Prep: 15 minutes   **Cook:** 30 minutes   **Cool:** 1 hour

1/10th of cake: 199 calories, 5g fat, 405mg sodium, 35.5g carbs, 1g fiber, 21g sugars, 4g protein

Ingredients

⅓ cup fat-free cream cheese
1 tablespoon Splenda No Calorie Sweetener (granulated)
⅓ cup Jet-Puffed Marshmallow Creme
⅛ teaspoon coconut extract
⅓ cup Cool Whip Free (thawed)
2 packets hot cocoa mix with 20 to 25 calories each
¼ cup mini semi-sweet chocolate chips
1 cup moist-style devil's food cake mix
1 cup moist-style yellow cake mix
½ cup fat-free liquid egg substitute
1 tablespoon red food coloring
⅛ teaspoon salt
¼ cup shredded sweetened coconut

Directions

Preheat oven to 350 degrees. Spray a 9-inch round cake pan with nonstick spray.

For a pic of this recipe, see the first photo insert. Yay!

In a medium bowl, thoroughly mix cream cheese with Splenda. Add marshmallow creme and coconut extract, and whisk vigorously until uniform. Add Cool Whip, and stir until uniform. Cover and refrigerate.

Place cocoa mix and 2 tablespoons chocolate chips in a glass. Add ½ cup very hot water, and stir until mostly dissolved. Add ½ cup cold water.

Transfer cocoa mixture to a large bowl. Add cake mixes, egg substitute, food coloring, and salt. Whisk until smooth.

Pour batter into the cake pan, and sprinkle with remaining 2 tablespoons chocolate chips.

Bake until a toothpick inserted into the center comes out mostly clean, 28 to 30 minutes.

Let cool completely, about 15 minutes in the pan and 45 minutes out of the pan on a cooling rack.

Plate cake, spread with cream cheese mixture, and sprinkle with shredded coconut. Devour!

MAKES 10 SERVINGS

199 calories per serving

CHEESECAKES

Cheesecake is SO decadent and almost always CRAZY RIDICULOUS when it comes to fat and calories. Well, we worked our faces off at the HG HQ to create the most AWESOME, creative, and decadently delicious no-guilt cheesecakes for you. And we were WILDLY successful . . . Enjoy!

CHEESECAKE 101!

* Because of the fat-free ingredients involved, your HG cheesecake will likely crack a little. Small price to pay for guilt-free cheesecake!

* To prevent *large* cracks from forming, it's important to start with room-temp ingredients. It generally takes at least 3 hours for the cream cheese to come to room temperature, so plan accordingly!

* Did you forget to bring your cream cheese to room temperature, or are you just in a hurry? Microwave it at 50 percent power in 10-second intervals. Alternate nuking and stirring until it just reaches room temp—don't overheat it!

* It's SUPER helpful to have all measured ingredients ready to go before you begin mixing. Set yourself up for success . . . Literally!

Banana Split Cheesecake

You'll Need: 9-inch springform cake pan, nonstick spray, large bowl, electric mixer

Prep: 15 minutes   **Cook:** 45 minutes   **Cool/Chill:** 3 hours

> **1/8th of cake:** 191 calories, 3g fat, 394mg sodium, 30g carbs, 1g fiber, 24g sugars, 11g protein

Ingredients

1 large ripe banana

16 ounces fat-free cream cheese, room temperature

½ cup granulated white sugar

½ teaspoon vanilla extract

¼ teaspoon banana extract

6 ounces (about ⅔ cup) fat-free vanilla Greek yogurt, room temperature

½ cup liquid egg whites (about 4 egg whites), room temperature

2 tablespoons all-purpose flour

¼ cup mini semi-sweet chocolate chips

8 maraschino cherries, blotted dry

No-Calorie Sweetener Alternative:

148 calories, 19g carbs, 11.5g sugars

Directions

Preheat oven to 350 degrees. Spray a 9-inch springform cake pan with nonstick spray.

Mash half of the banana. Refrigerate the other half until ready to serve.

Combine cream cheese, sugar, vanilla extract, and banana extract in a large bowl. With an electric mixer set to medium speed, beat until smooth, 1 to 2 minutes.

Continue to beat the mixture while gradually adding yogurt, egg whites, flour, and mashed banana. Beat until uniform, about 2 minutes.

Evenly pour batter into the cake pan. Sprinkle with chocolate chips.

Bake until firm, 40 to 45 minutes.

Let cool completely, about 2 hours.

Refrigerate until chilled, at least 1 hour.

Just before serving, thinly slice the remaining half of the banana into coins. Evenly top cheesecake with banana coins and cherries.

Release springform, and serve!

MAKES 8 SERVINGS

191 calories per serving

Super-Strawberry Cheesecake

You'll Need: 9-inch springform cake pan, nonstick spray, large bowl, electric mixer, medium nonstick pot, medium bowl

Prep: 20 minutes   **Cook:** 1 hour   **Cool/Chill:** 3 hours

1/8th of cake: 161 calories, 1g fat, 415mg sodium, 27g carbs, 1g fiber, 21g sugars, 11g protein

Ingredients

Cheesecake
16 ounces fat-free cream cheese, room temperature

½ cup granulated white sugar

1 teaspoon vanilla extract

6 ounces (about ⅔ cup) fat-free vanilla Greek yogurt, room temperature

½ cup liquid egg whites (about 4 egg whites), room temperature

2 tablespoons lemon juice, room temperature

2 tablespoons all-purpose flour

¼ teaspoon cinnamon

Topping
1 tablespoon cornstarch

2 cups frozen unsweetened strawberries, partially thawed and sliced

2 tablespoons granulated white sugar

¼ teaspoon cinnamon

Dash salt

No-Calorie Sweetener Alternative:

109 calories, 13g carbs, 5.5g sugars

For a pic of this recipe, see the first photo insert. Yay!

Directions

Preheat oven to 350 degrees. Spray a 9-inch springform cake pan with nonstick spray.

In a large bowl, combine cream cheese, sugar, and vanilla extract. With an electric mixer set to medium speed, beat until smooth, 1 to 2 minutes.

Continue to beat while gradually adding yogurt, egg whites, lemon juice, flour, and cinnamon. Beat until uniform, about 2 minutes.

Evenly pour mixture into the cake pan.

Bake until firm, 40 to 45 minutes.

Let cool completely, about 2 hours.

Meanwhile, in a medium nonstick pot, combine cornstarch with ½ cup cold water, and stir to dissolve. Add remaining topping ingredients, and mix well. Set heat to medium. Stirring frequently, cook until thick and gooey, 12 to 14 minutes. Transfer to a medium bowl, and let cool completely.

Evenly pour topping over the cheesecake in the pan. Refrigerate until chilled, at least 1 hour.

Once ready to serve, release springform, and dig in!

MAKES 8 SERVINGS

HG Tip!

The topping may run down the edges of the cake once the springform is removed. To catch all of that deliciousness, place the pan on a large plate before removing the springform.

Strawberry Upside-Down
Cheesecake Squares

You'll Need: 8-inch by 8-inch baking pan, nonstick spray, medium microwave-safe bowl, large bowl, electric mixer

Prep: 15 minutes   **Cook:** 1 hour   **Cool/Chill:** 3 hours

> **1/9ᵗʰ of recipe:** 142 calories, 1g fat, 361mg sodium, 23g carbs, 0.5g fiber, 18g sugars, 9.5g protein

Ingredients

1 cup frozen unsweetened strawberries
¼ cup low-sugar strawberry preserves
16 ounces fat-free cream cheese, room temperature
½ cup granulated white sugar
1 teaspoon vanilla extract
6 ounces (about ⅔ cup) fat-free vanilla Greek yogurt, room temperature
½ cup liquid egg whites (about 4 egg whites), room temperature
2 tablespoons lemon juice, room temperature
2 tablespoons all-purpose flour
¼ teaspoon cinnamon
1 sheet (4 crackers) low-fat honey graham crackers, crushed

No-Calorie Sweetener Alternative:

104 calories, 13g carbs, 7g sugars

Directions

Preheat oven to 350 degrees. Spray an 8-inch by 8-inch baking pan with nonstick spray.

In a medium microwave-safe bowl, microwave strawberries until thawed, about 1 minute. Do not drain excess liquid. Add preserves, and thoroughly mash with a fork.

In a large bowl, combine cream cheese, sugar, and vanilla extract. With an electric mixer set to medium speed, beat until smooth, 1 to 2 minutes.

Continue to beat while gradually adding strawberry mixture, yogurt, egg whites, lemon juice, flour, and cinnamon. Beat until uniform, about 2 minutes.

Evenly pour mixture into the baking pan. Bake until firm, about 1 hour.

Let cool completely, about 2 hours.

Refrigerate until chilled, at least 1 hour.

Sprinkle with crushed grahams. Enjoy!

MAKES 9 SERVINGS

142 calories per serving

✳ Flip to the photo inserts to see dozens of recipe pics! And for photos of ALL the recipes, go to **hungry-girl.com/books**.

Chocolate Chip Candy Cane Cheesecake

You'll Need: 9-inch springform cake pan, nonstick spray, large bowl, electric mixer

Prep: 15 minutes   **Cook:** 45 minutes   **Cool/Chill:** 3 hours

⅛th of cake: 181 calories, 3g fat, 395mg sodium, 27.5g carbs, 0.5g fiber, 23g sugars, 11g protein

Ingredients

16 ounces fat-free cream cheese, room temperature

½ cup granulated white sugar

1 teaspoon vanilla extract

6 ounces (about ⅔ cup) fat-free vanilla Greek yogurt, room temperature

½ cup liquid egg whites (about 4 egg whites), room temperature

2 tablespoons all-purpose flour

2 standard-sized candy canes or 8 mini candy canes, crushed

¼ cup mini semi-sweet chocolate chips

Optional topping: Fat Free Reddi-wip

No-Calorie Sweetener Alternative:

138 calories, 16.5g carbs, 10.5g sugars

Directions

Preheat oven to 350 degrees. Spray a 9-inch springform cake pan with nonstick spray.

In a large bowl, combine cream cheese, sugar, and vanilla extract. With an electric mixer set to medium speed, beat until smooth, 1 to 2 minutes.

Continue to beat while gradually adding yogurt, egg whites, and flour. Beat until uniform, about 2 minutes.

Stir in half of the crushed candy canes. Evenly pour mixture into the cake pan.

Sprinkle with chocolate chips. Bake until firm, 40 to 45 minutes.

Sprinkle with remaining crushed candy canes.

Let cool completely, about 2 hours.

Refrigerate until chilled, at least 1 hour.

Release springform, slice, and serve!

MAKES 8 SERVINGS

181 calories per serving

Grasshopper Cheesecake

You'll Need: 9-inch springform cake pan, nonstick spray, large bowl, electric mixer

Prep: 15 minutes   **Cook:** 45 minutes   **Cool/Chill:** 3 hours

1/8th of cake: 157 calories, 2.5g fat, 405mg sodium, 23.5g carbs, <0.5g fiber, 18.5g sugars, 11g protein

Ingredients

16 ounces fat-free cream cheese, room temperature
½ cup granulated white sugar
¾ teaspoon vanilla extract
¼ teaspoon peppermint extract
4 drops green food coloring
6 ounces (about ⅔ cup) fat-free vanilla Greek yogurt, room temperature
½ cup liquid egg whites (about 4 egg whites), room temperature
2 tablespoons all-purpose flour
2 tablespoons mini semi-sweet chocolate chips
1 sheet (4 crackers) chocolate graham crackers, crushed

No-Calorie Sweetener Alternative:

115 calories, 12.5g carbs, 6g sugars

Directions

Preheat oven to 350 degrees. Spray a 9-inch springform cake pan with nonstick spray.

In a large bowl, combine cream cheese, sugar, vanilla extract, peppermint extract, and food coloring. With an electric mixer set to medium speed, beat until smooth, 1 to 2 minutes.

Continue to beat while gradually adding yogurt, egg whites, and flour. Beat until uniform, about 2 minutes.

Evenly pour mixture into the cake pan. Sprinkle with chocolate chips.

Bake until firm, 40 to 45 minutes.

Let cool completely, about 2 hours.

Refrigerate until chilled, about 1 hour.

Sprinkle with crushed grahams. Release springform, slice, and enjoy!

MAKES 8 SERVINGS

157 calories per serving

For more recipes, tips & tricks, sign up for FREE daily emails at hungry-girl.com!

Mini PB&J Cheesecakes

You'll Need: 12-cup muffin pan, foil baking cups, large bowl, electric mixer

Prep: 20 minutes   **Cook:** 20 minutes   **Cool/Chill:** 1½ hours

1/12ᵗʰ of recipe (1 mini cheesecake): 166 calories, 4.5g fat, 327mg sodium, 20g carbs, 0.5g fiber, 14g sugars, 10g protein

Ingredients

16 ounces fat-free cream cheese,
    room temperature

½ cup reduced-fat creamy peanut butter

½ cup granulated white sugar

1 teaspoon vanilla extract

6 ounces (about ⅔ cup) fat-free vanilla
    Greek yogurt, room temperature

¾ cup liquid egg whites (about 6 egg whites),
    room temperature

2 tablespoons all-purpose flour

⅓ cup low-sugar strawberry or grape preserves

**No-Calorie
Sweetener Alternative:**

138 calories, 13g carbs,
5.5g sugars

Directions

Preheat oven to 350 degrees. Line a 12-cup muffin pan with foil baking cups.

In a large bowl, combine cream cheese, peanut butter, sugar, and vanilla extract. With an electric mixer set to medium speed, beat until smooth, 1 to 2 minutes.

Continue to beat while gradually adding yogurt, egg whites, and flour. Beat until uniform, about 2 minutes.

Evenly distribute batter among the cups of the muffin pan. (Cups will be very full!) Bake until firm, about 20 minutes.

Let cool completely, about 10 minutes in the pan and 50 minutes out of the pan.

Top with preserves, and refrigerate until chilled, at least 30 minutes. Eat up!

MAKES 12 SERVINGS

166 calories per serving

Hungry for More?

Flip to page 363 for ALL the cheesecake creations!

CHAPTER 5

BROWNIES & FUDGE

Brownies and fudge are like royalty in the dessert world!
Chocolate fanatics: Make sure you're sitting down . . .

BROWNIES

What can we say? We went a little BONKERS with the brownies here . . . but we had no choice. We're good at this stuff—and people LOVE brownies and DEMAND creative brownie recipes. It'll be hard to pick your favorite . . . but the good news is, it's okay to love 'em all!

BROWNIE BASICS . . .

HG brownies are made with canned pure pumpkin, but they taste 100 percent chocolatey! The pumpkin just makes 'em moist and eliminates the need for butter, eggs, oil, etc.

Beware of pure pumpkin's doppelganger, canned pumpkin pie filling. The cans look similar, but pumpkin pie filling has more than twice as many calories and over three times as much sugar as pumpkin puree.

Your brownie batter will be thick, and you may be tempted to add other ingredients like the ones mentioned on the cake mix boxes. Don't do it! Just mix until as smooth as possible.

HG brownies taste great when chilled. They're more fudgy that way!

Caramel White Chocolate Brownies

You'll Need: 9-inch by 13-inch baking pan, nonstick spray, large bowl

Prep: 15 minutes   **Cook:** 20 minutes   **Cool:** 1½ hours

> **1/16th of recipe:** 151 calories, 3g fat, 270mg sodium, 30g carbs, 1.5g fiber, 17g sugars, 2g protein

Ingredients

1 box moist-style devil's food cake mix (15.25 to 18.25 ounces)
One 15-ounce can pure pumpkin
¼ cup fat-free, low-fat, or light caramel dip
3 tablespoons white chocolate chips, chopped

Directions

Preheat oven to 400 degrees. Spray a 9-inch by 13-inch baking pan with nonstick spray.

In a large bowl, mix cake mix with pumpkin until smooth and uniform. Spread batter into the baking pan, and smooth out the top.

Bake until a toothpick inserted into the center comes out clean, 18 to 20 minutes.

Let cool completely, about 1½ hours.

Drizzle brownies with caramel, and sprinkle with chopped white chocolate chips. Serve and enjoy!

MAKES 16 SERVINGS

S'mores Brownies

You'll Need: 9-inch by 13-inch baking pan, nonstick spray, large bowl, medium bowl

Prep: 15 minutes   **Cook:** 20 minutes   **Cool:** 1½ hours

> **1/16th of recipe:** 146 calories, 2.5g fat, 268mg sodium, 30g carbs, 2g fiber, 16.5g sugars, 2g protein

calories per serving

146

Ingredients

1 box moist-style devil's food cake mix (15.25 to 18.25 ounces)
One 15-ounce can pure pumpkin
½ cup Jet-Puffed Marshmallow Creme
2 teaspoons light vanilla soymilk
2 sheets (8 crackers) low-fat honey graham crackers, roughly crushed
1 tablespoon mini semi-sweet chocolate chips

HG Alternative: Feel free to use milk or your milk swap of choice in place of the soymilk. It'll barely affect the taste or nutritionals.

Directions

Preheat oven to 400 degrees. Spray a 9-inch by 13-inch baking pan with nonstick spray.

In a large bowl, mix cake mix with pumpkin until smooth and uniform. Spread batter into the baking pan, and smooth out the top.

Bake until a toothpick inserted into the center comes out clean, 18 to 20 minutes.

Let cool completely, about 1½ hours.

In a medium bowl, mix marshmallow creme with soymilk until uniform.

Drizzle brownies with marshmallow creme mixture, and sprinkle with crushed graham crackers and chocolate chips. Serve and enjoy!

MAKES 16 SERVINGS

Fudgy Frosted Walnut Brownies

You'll Need: 9-inch by 13-inch baking pan, nonstick spray, medium bowl, large bowl

Prep: 15 minutes   **Cook:** 20 minutes   **Cool:** 1½ hours

> **1/16th of recipe:** 172 calories, 5.5g fat, 277mg sodium, 29.5g carbs, 2g fiber, 16.5g sugars, 2.5g protein

Ingredients

⅓ cup chocolate frosting
1 sugar-free chocolate pudding snack with 60 calories or less
1 box moist-style devil's food cake mix (15.25 to 18.25 ounces)
One 15-ounce can pure pumpkin
½ cup chopped walnuts

Directions

Preheat oven to 400 degrees. Spray a 9-inch by 13-inch baking pan with nonstick spray.

In a medium bowl, mix frosting with pudding until smooth and uniform. Cover and refrigerate.

In a large bowl, mix cake mix with pumpkin until smooth and uniform. Spread batter into the baking pan, and smooth out the top.

Bake until a toothpick inserted into the center comes out clean, 18 to 20 minutes.

Let cool completely, about 1½ hours.

Spread brownies with frosting mixture, and sprinkle with walnuts. Mmmm!

MAKES 16 SERVINGS

172 _calories per serving_

Swirly Chocolate-Cheesecake Brownies

You'll Need: 9-inch by 13-inch baking pan, nonstick spray, 2 large bowls

Prep: 15 minutes   **Cook:** 20 minutes   **Cool:** 1½ hours

1/16ᵗʰ of recipe: 148 calories, 2.5g fat, 364mg sodium, 28.5g carbs, 2g fiber, 16.5g sugars, 3.5g protein

Ingredients

1 box moist-style devil's food cake mix
   (15.25 to 18.25 ounces)
One 15-ounce can pure pumpkin
One 8-ounce container fat-free cream cheese
2 tablespoons granulated white sugar
2 packets hot cocoa mix with
   20 to 25 calories each
2 tablespoons light chocolate syrup
¼ teaspoon vanilla extract

No-Calorie Sweetener Alternative:

143 calories, 27.5g carbs, 15g sugars

Directions

Preheat oven to 400 degrees. Spray a 9-inch by 13-inch baking pan with nonstick spray.

In a large bowl, mix cake mix with pumpkin until smooth and uniform. Spread batter into the baking pan, and smooth out the top.

In another large bowl, combine cream cheese with sugar, and stir until smooth. Add hot cocoa mix, chocolate syrup, and vanilla extract. Stir until smooth.

Spoon cream cheese mixture over the batter, and use a knife to swirl it in.

Bake until a toothpick inserted into the center comes out mostly clean, 18 to 20 minutes.

Let cool completely, about 1½ hours. Serve and enjoy!

MAKES 16 SERVINGS

148 calories per serving

Candy Cane Brownies

156 calories per serving

You'll Need: 9-inch by 13-inch baking pan, nonstick spray, medium bowl, large bowl

Prep: 15 minutes   **Cook:** 20 minutes   **Cool:** 1½ hours

> **1/16th of recipe:** 156 calories, 3g fat, 278mg sodium, 30.5g carbs, 2g fiber, 17.5g sugars, 2g protein

Ingredients

⅓ cup chocolate frosting
1 sugar-free chocolate pudding snack with 60 calories or less
1 box moist-style devil's food cake mix (15.25 to 18.25 ounces)
One 15-ounce can pure pumpkin
¼ teaspoon peppermint extract
2 standard-sized candy canes or 8 mini candy canes

Directions

Preheat oven to 400 degrees. Spray a 9-inch by 13-inch baking pan with nonstick spray.

In a medium bowl, mix frosting with pudding until smooth and uniform. Cover and refrigerate.

In a large bowl, mix cake mix, pumpkin, and peppermint extract until smooth and uniform. Finely crush half of the candy canes, and stir into the batter. Spread batter into the baking pan.

Bake until a toothpick inserted into the center comes out mostly clean, 18 to 20 minutes.

Let cool completely, about 1½ hours.

Spread brownies with frosting mixture. Just before serving, roughly crush the remaining candy canes, and sprinkle over brownies. Enjoy!

MAKES 16 SERVINGS

Chocolate Amaze-mint Brownies

You'll Need: 9-inch by 13-inch baking pan, nonstick spray, large bowl

Prep: 15 minutes   **Cook:** 20 minutes   **Cool:** 1½ hours

> **1/16th of recipe:** 141 calories, 2.5g fat, 254mg sodium, 29g carbs, 2g fiber, 16.5g sugars, 2g protein

Ingredients

1 box moist-style devil's food cake mix (15.25 to 18.25 ounces)
One 15-ounce can pure pumpkin
½ teaspoon peppermint extract
2 standard-sized York Peppermint Patties (1.4 ounces each)

Directions

Preheat oven to 400 degrees. Spray a 9-inch by 13-inch baking pan with nonstick spray.

In a large bowl, combine cake mix, pumpkin, and peppermint extract. Mix until smooth and uniform. Spread batter into the baking pan, and smooth out the top.

Bake until a toothpick inserted into the center comes out clean, 18 to 20 minutes.

Finely chop peppermint patties. Evenly distribute over the brownies, and pat to adhere.

Let cool completely, about 1½ hours. Dig in!

MAKES 16 SERVINGS

141
calories per serving

PB Banana Brownies

You'll Need: 9-inch by 13-inch baking pan, nonstick spray, large bowl, small bowl

Prep: 20 minutes **Cook:** 25 minutes **Cool:** 1½ hours

1/16th of recipe: 158 calories, 3.5g fat, 274mg sodium, 29.5g carbs, 2g fiber, 15g sugars, 3g protein

Ingredients

1 box moist-style devil's food cake mix (15.25 to 18.25 ounces)
1 cup canned pure pumpkin
1 cup mashed ripe banana
¼ cup creamy reduced-fat peanut butter
1 tablespoon light vanilla soymilk

Directions

Preheat oven to 400 degrees. Spray a 9-inch by 13-inch baking pan with nonstick spray.

In a large bowl, combine cake mix, pumpkin, and banana. Mix until smooth and uniform. Spread batter into the baking pan, and smooth out the top.

In a small bowl, mix peanut butter with soymilk until smooth and uniform.

Spoon peanut butter mixture over the batter, and use a knife to swirl it in.

Bake until a toothpick inserted into the center comes out clean, 20 to 22 minutes.

Let cool completely, about 1½ hours. Eat up!

MAKES 16 SERVINGS

Snickers Madness Brownies

You'll Need: 9-inch by 13-inch baking pan, nonstick spray, large bowl

Prep: 15 minutes   **Cook:** 20 minutes   **Cool:** 1½ hours

> **1/16th of recipe:** 158 calories, 3.5g fat, 285mg sodium, 30g carbs, 2g fiber, 16.5g sugars, 2.5g protein

Ingredients

1 box moist-style devil's food cake mix (15.25 to 18.25 ounces)
One 15-ounce can pure pumpkin
¼ cup fat-free, low-fat, or light caramel dip
¼ cup chopped peanuts
2 tablespoons mini semi-sweet chocolate chips

Directions

Preheat oven to 400 degrees. Spray a 9-inch by 13-inch baking pan with nonstick spray.

In a large bowl, mix cake mix with pumpkin until smooth and uniform. Spread batter into the baking pan, and smooth out the top.

Bake until a toothpick inserted into the center comes out clean, 18 to 20 minutes.

Let cool completely, about 1½ hours.

Drizzle brownies with caramel, and sprinkle with peanuts and chocolate chips. Yum!

MAKES 16 SERVINGS

For a pic of this recipe, see the first photo insert. Yay!

158 calories per serving

Cookies 'n Cream Brownies

You'll Need: 9-inch by 13-inch baking pan, nonstick spray, large bowl, small microwave-safe bowl

Prep: 15 minutes   **Cook:** 20 minutes   **Cool:** 1½ hours

1/16th of recipe: 146 calories, 2.5g fat, 273mg sodium, 29.5g carbs, 2g fiber, 15.5g sugars, 2g protein

Ingredients

1 box moist-style devil's food cake mix (15.25 to 18.25 ounces)
One 15-ounce can pure pumpkin
6 Reduced Fat Oreo cookies, roughly crushed
1 teaspoon cornstarch
1 tablespoon powdered sugar
1 drop vanilla extract
1 tablespoon Jet-Puffed Marshmallow Creme
1 tablespoon Cool Whip Free (thawed)

Directions

Preheat oven to 400 degrees. Spray a 9-inch by 13-inch baking pan with nonstick spray.

In a large bowl, mix cake mix with pumpkin until smooth and uniform. Spread batter into the baking pan, and smooth out the top.

Sprinkle with crushed cookies. Bake until a toothpick inserted into the center comes out clean, 18 to 20 minutes.

For a pic of this recipe, see the first photo insert. Yay!

Let cool completely, about 1½ hours.

Meanwhile, to make the icing, in a small microwave-safe bowl, combine cornstarch with ½ tablespoon cold water, and stir to dissolve. Add powdered sugar and vanilla extract, and mix well. Add marshmallow creme and microwave for 5 seconds, or until creme is very soft. Stir until smooth. Stir in Cool Whip. Cover and refrigerate.

Drizzle brownies with icing, and enjoy!

MAKES 16 SERVINGS

146 calories per serving

For more recipes, tips & tricks, sign up for FREE daily emails at **hungry-girl.com!**

Caramel-PB Brownies

149 calories per serving

You'll Need: 9-inch by 13-inch baking pan, nonstick spray, large bowl, small bowl

Prep: 15 minutes   **Cook:** 20 minutes   **Cool:** 1½ hours

1/16th of recipe: 149 calories, 3g fat, 277mg sodium, 28g carbs, 2g fiber, 15g sugars, 2.5g protein

Ingredients

1 box moist-style devil's food cake mix (15.25 to 18.25 ounces)
One 15-ounce can pure pumpkin
3 tablespoons creamy reduced-fat peanut butter
2 tablespoons fat-free, low-fat, or light caramel dip
2 tablespoons light vanilla soymilk

Directions

Preheat oven to 400 degrees. Spray a 9-inch by 13-inch baking pan with nonstick spray.

In a large bowl, mix cake mix with pumpkin until smooth and uniform. Spread batter into the baking pan, and smooth out the top.

Bake until a toothpick inserted into the center comes out clean, 18 to 20 minutes.

Let cool completely, about 1½ hours.

In a small bowl, combine peanut butter, caramel dip, and soymilk. Vigorously stir until smooth and uniform.

Drizzle brownies with peanut butter mixture. Mmmm!

MAKES 16 SERVINGS

Yum Yum Red Velvet Brownie Muffins

You'll Need: 12-cup muffin pan, foil baking cups or nonstick spray, large bowl, whisk

Prep: 10 minutes   **Cook:** 20 minutes   **Cool:** 30 minutes

> **1/12th of recipe (1 muffin):** 192 calories, 4.5g fat, 261mg sodium, 35.5g carbs, 1.5g fiber, 20g sugars, 2.5g protein

Ingredients

One 18.25-ounce box Duncan Hines Signature Red Velvet Cake Mix
One 15-ounce can pure pumpkin

Directions

Preheat oven to 375 degrees. Line a 12-cup muffin pan with foil baking cups, or spray it with nonstick spray.

In a large bowl, whisk cake mix until mostly free of lumps. Add pumpkin, and mix until smooth and uniform.

Evenly distribute batter into the cups of the muffin pan. Bake until a toothpick inserted into the center of a muffin comes out mostly clean, about 20 minutes.

Let cool completely, about 10 minutes in the pan and 20 minutes out of the pan.

MAKES 12 SERVINGS

HG FYI:
This batter is SUPER thick! Just mix until it's as smooth as possible!

Black Forest Brownies

You'll Need: 9-inch by 13-inch baking pan, nonstick spray, large bowl, medium nonstick pot, medium bowl

Prep: 15 minutes   **Cook:** 30 minutes   **Cool:** 1½ hours

> **1/16th of recipe:** 141 calories, 2g fat, 268mg sodium, 29g carbs, 2g fiber, 15.5g sugars, 2g protein

Ingredients

1 box moist-style devil's food cake mix
     (15.25 to 18.25 ounces)
One 15-ounce can pure pumpkin
1½ tablespoons cornstarch
2 cups frozen unsweetened pitted dark sweet
     cherries, partially thawed and chopped
⅓ cup Splenda No Calorie Sweetener (granulated)
½ teaspoon lemon juice
⅛ teaspoon cinnamon
⅛ teaspoon salt

Sugar Alternative:

155 calories, 33g carbs, 20g sugars

Directions

Preheat oven to 400 degrees. Spray a 9-inch by 13-inch baking pan with nonstick spray.

In a large bowl, mix cake mix with pumpkin until smooth and uniform. Spread batter into the baking pan, and smooth out the top.

Bake until a toothpick inserted into the center comes out clean, 18 to 20 minutes.

Let cool completely, about 1½ hours.

Meanwhile, in a medium nonstick pot, combine cornstarch with ¼ cup cold water, and stir to dissolve. Add remaining ingredients, and stir well. Set heat to medium. Stirring frequently, cook until mixture is thick and gooey, 8 to 10 minutes. Transfer to a medium bowl, and let cool completely.

Evenly top brownies with cherry mixture. Enjoy!

MAKES 16 SERVINGS

141 calories per serving

Hungry for More?

Check out these terrific brownie treats!

* Walnut Brownie Pops (page 72)
* Brownie Sundae Cupcakes (page 210)
* Brownie-Bottomed Ice Cream Cake (page 220)

And don't miss page 357 for ALL the chocolate desserts!

FUDGE

Hungry Girl fudge is unique. If you haven't tried it, you should. It won't taste EXACTLY like the fudge you may be used to, since it's made with pumpkin instead of cream and butter. But we figure you'd rather have a face full of special HG fudge than have too-tight pants. (We're right, right?!)

THE FUDGE 411!

* The cooked batter might appear to be undercooked at first. We promise, it'll firm up after cooling!

* For the perfect consistency, let the fudge cool and chill *completely* before you cut into it. This takes about 6 hours—not speedy, but worth the wait!

* If you refrigerate your fudge before it's cooled, a layer of condensation may form and interfere with the firming process. Don't do it!

Salted Caramel Fudge

You'll Need: 8-inch by 8-inch baking pan, nonstick spray, large bowl

Prep: 10 minutes   **Cook:** 45 minutes   **Cool/Chill:** 6 hours

1/36th of recipe: 68 calories, 1g fat, 107mg sodium, 15g carbs, 0.5g fiber, 10.5g sugars, 0.5g protein

Ingredients

1 box fudge brownie mix (18.3 - 19.5 ounces)
2 cups canned pure pumpkin
2 tablespoons light chocolate syrup
¼ cup fat-free, low-fat, or light caramel dip
1 teaspoon coarse sea salt

Directions

Preheat oven to 350 degrees. Spray an 8-inch by 8-inch baking pan with nonstick spray.

In a large bowl, combine brownie mix, pumpkin, and chocolate syrup. Mix until smooth and uniform. Spread batter into the baking pan, and smooth out the top.

Bake until edges are slightly firm and top center is dry to the touch, 40 to 45 minutes.

Let cool completely, about 4 hours.

Drizzle fudge with caramel dip. Refrigerate until chilled, at least 2 hours.

Just before serving, sprinkle with salt. Mmmm!

MAKES 36 SERVINGS

For a pic of this recipe, see the first photo insert. Yay!

68 calories per serving

Crazy for Coconut Fudge

You'll Need: 8-inch by 8-inch baking pan, nonstick spray, large bowl

Prep: 10 minutes   **Cook:** 45 minutes   **Cool/Chill:** 6 hours

> **1/36th of recipe:** 68 calories, 1g fat, 50mg sodium, 14g carbs, 0.5g fiber, 10g sugars, 0.5g protein

68 calories per serving

Ingredients

1 box fudge brownie mix (18.3 - 19.5 ounces)
2 cups canned pure pumpkin
2 tablespoons light chocolate syrup
1 ½ teaspoons coconut extract
⅓ cup shredded sweetened coconut

Directions

Preheat oven to 350 degrees. Spray an 8-inch by 8-inch baking pan with nonstick spray.

In a large bowl, combine brownie mix, pumpkin, chocolate syrup, and coconut extract. Mix until smooth and uniform. Spread batter into the baking pan, and smooth out the top.

Bake until edges are slightly firm and top center is dry to the touch, 40 to 45 minutes.

Sprinkle with shredded coconut, and pat to adhere.

Let cool completely, about 4 hours.

Refrigerate until chilled, at least 2 hours. Go cocoNUTS!

MAKES 36 SERVINGS

Bacon Maple Madness Fudge

You'll Need: 8-inch by 8-inch baking pan, nonstick spray, large bowl

Prep: 10 minutes **Cook:** 45 minutes **Cool/Chill:** 6 hours

> **1/36th of recipe:** 68 calories, 1g fat, 89mg sodium, 13.5g carbs, 0.5g fiber, 9.5g sugars, 1g protein

Ingredients

1 box fudge brownie mix (18.3 - 19.5 ounces)
2 cups canned pure pumpkin
2 tablespoons light chocolate syrup
1½ teaspoons maple extract
½ cup precooked real crumbled bacon

Directions

Preheat oven to 350 degrees. Spray an 8-inch by 8-inch baking pan with nonstick spray.

In a large bowl, combine brownie mix, pumpkin, syrup, and maple extract. Mix until smooth and uniform. Spread batter into the baking pan, and smooth out the top.

Sprinkle with bacon. Bake until edges are slightly firm and top center of fudge is dry to the touch, 40 to 45 minutes.

Let cool completely, about 4 hours.

Refrigerate until chilled, at least 2 hours. Devour!

MAKES 36 SERVINGS

68 calories per serving

Nutty-Good Fudge

You'll Need: 8-inch by 8-inch baking pan, nonstick spray, large bowl

Prep: 10 minutes   **Cook:** 45 minutes   **Cool/Chill:** 6 hours

1/36th of recipe: 72 calories, 2g fat, 47mg sodium, 14g carbs, 0.5g fiber, 9.5g sugars, 0.5g protein

Ingredients

1 box fudge brownie mix (18.3 - 19.5 ounces)
2 cups canned pure pumpkin
2 tablespoons light chocolate syrup
⅓ cup plus 2 tablespoons chopped walnuts

Directions

Preheat oven to 350 degrees. Spray an 8-inch by 8-inch baking pan with nonstick spray.

In a large bowl, combine brownie mix, pumpkin, and chocolate syrup. Mix until smooth and uniform.

Stir in ⅓ cup walnuts. Spread batter into the baking pan, and smooth out the top.

Sprinkle with remaining 2 tablespoons walnuts. Bake until edges are slightly firm and top center is dry to the touch, 40 to 45 minutes.

Let cool completely, about 4 hours.

Refrigerate until chilled, at least 2 hours. Enjoy!

MAKES 36 SERVINGS

CHAPTER 6

PIES & CUTIE PIES

Fruit pies, cream pies, huge pies, itty-bitty pies . . .
They're ALL here. YAY!!!!!

Kickin' Key Lime Pie

You'll Need: 9-inch pie pan, nonstick spray, blender or food processor, medium bowl, small microwave-safe bowl, large bowl, whisk

Prep: 20 minutes   **Cook:** 25 minutes   **Cool/Chill:** 3 hours

1/8th of pie: 182 calories, 4.5g fat, 169mg sodium, 34g carbs, 3.5g fiber, 21.5g sugars, 5g protein

Ingredients

Crust
1 cup Fiber One Original bran cereal

2 sheets (8 crackers) low-fat honey graham crackers, broken into pieces

3 tablespoons Splenda No Calorie Sweetener (granulated)

¼ cup light whipped butter or light buttery spread

Filling
¾ cup fat-free sweetened condensed milk

½ cup lime juice (preferably key lime)

½ cup light sour cream

¼ cup fat-free liquid egg substitute

Topping
1 cup Cool Whip Free (thawed)

Optional: lime zest (preferably key lime)

Sugar Alternative:

197 calories, 38g carbs, 26g sugars

For a pic of this recipe, see the first photo insert. Yay!

Super-Strawberry Cheesecake, p. 108

161 calories PER SERVING

CAKE MUGS & MORE DESSERTS IN A MUG

Streusel-Topped Pumpkin Pie in a Mug, p. 26

Peach Crisp in a Mug, p. 25

Chunky Monkey Cake Mug, p. 14

135 calories PER SERVING

Tie-Dye-For Cupcakes, p. 48

148 calories PER SERVING

Apple Streusel Cupcakes, p. 52

154 calories PER SERVING

PB Cheesecake Chocolate Cupcakes, p. 44

110 calories PER SERVING

Pumpkin Pie Cupcakes, p. 50

CAKE POPS

110 calories PER SERVING

Walnut Brownie Pops, p. 72

90 calories PER SERVING

Birthday Cake Pops, p. 84

101 calories PER SERVING

Chocolate PB Cake Pops, p. 86

CAKES & CHEESECAKES * BROWNIES & FUDGE

Red Velvet Coconut Cream Cake, p. 102

Salted Caramel Fudge, p. 137

Snickers Madness Brownies, p. 129

Cookies 'n Cream Brownies, p. 130

Vanilla Caramel Dream Cake, p. 98

PIES & CUTIE PIES

Yummy Crumbly Lemon Meringue Pie, p. 148

Banana Cream Cutie Pies, p. 160

Kickin' Key Lime Pie, p. 144

108 calories PER SERVING

Mini Red Velvet Cheesecake Whoopie Pies, p. 192

185 calories PER SERVING

PB&J Softies, p. 172

135 calories PER SERVING

Pretzel Chocolate Softies, p. 168

Too-Cool Mint Chocolate Whoopie Pies, p. 189

153
calories
PER SERVING

Directions

Preheat oven to 350 degrees. Spray a 9-inch pie pan with nonstick spray.

To make the crust, in a blender or food processor, grind cereal and graham cracker pieces into crumbs. Transfer to a medium bowl, and mix in Splenda.

Place butter in a small microwave-safe bowl. Add 2 tablespoons water, and microwave for 30 seconds, or until butter has melted. Add mixture to the medium bowl, and thoroughly mix.

Evenly distribute mixture along the bottom of the pie pan, and firmly press to form the crust. Press it into the edges and up along the sides of the pan.

Bake until firm, about 10 minutes. Remove pan, but leave oven on.

In a large bowl, combine condensed milk, lime juice, and sour cream. Whisk thoroughly. Add egg substitute, and gently mix until uniform.

Spread filling into the crust. Bake until edges are firm, about 15 minutes.

Let cool completely, about 1½ hours.

Refrigerate until chilled, at least 1½ hours.

Just before serving, top each slice with a 2-tablespoon dollop of Cool Whip. Enjoy!

MAKES 8 SERVINGS

182 calories per serving

True Blueberry Pie

You'll Need: 9-inch pie pan, nonstick spray, blender or food processor, medium bowl, small microwave-safe bowl, large nonstick pot

Prep: 15 minutes   **Cook:** 25 minutes   **Cool/Chill:** 2 hours

1/8th of pie: 120 calories, 3.5g fat, 168mg sodium, 25g carbs, 5.5g fiber, 8.5g sugars, 1.5g protein

Ingredients

Crust
1 cup Fiber One Original bran cereal
2 sheets (8 crackers) low-fat honey graham crackers, broken into pieces
3 tablespoons Splenda No Calorie Sweetener (granulated)
¼ teaspoon cinnamon
¼ cup light whipped butter or light buttery spread

Filling
3 tablespoons cornstarch
4 cups blueberries
⅔ cup Splenda No Calorie Sweetener (granulated)
1 teaspoon lemon juice
¼ teaspoon cinnamon
¼ teaspoon salt

Optional topping: Fat Free Reddi-wip

HG Alternative: Use frozen berries! Thaw them, but don't drain the excess liquid. (The berries might not soften and burst, but the mixture will thicken and the pie will taste great!)

Sugar Alternative:

191 calories, 44g carbs, 29.5g sugars

Directions

Preheat oven to 350 degrees. Spray a 9-inch pie pan with nonstick spray.

To make the crust, in a blender or food processor, grind cereal and graham cracker pieces into crumbs. Transfer to a medium bowl, and mix in Splenda and cinnamon.

Place butter in a small microwave-safe bowl. Add 2 tablespoons water, and microwave for 30 seconds, or until butter has melted. Add mixture to the medium bowl, and thoroughly mix.

Evenly distribute crust mixture along the bottom of the pie pan, and firmly press to form the crust. Press it into the edges and up along the sides of the pan.

Bake until firm, about 10 minutes.

To make the filling, place cornstarch in a large nonstick pot. Add ½ cup cold water, and stir to dissolve. Add remaining ingredients, and mix well.

Set heat to medium. Stirring frequently, cook until berries have softened and burst and mixture has thickened, 10 to 12 minutes.

Carefully transfer filling to the pie pan.

Let cool and set completely, about 1 hour.

Refrigerate until chilled, at least 1 hour. Eat up!

MAKES 8 SERVINGS

120 calories per serving

Yummy Crumbly Lemon Meringue Pie

You'll Need: 9-inch pie pan, nonstick spray, blender or food processor, medium bowl, small microwave-safe bowl, medium-large bowl, small nonstick pot, whisk, large metal or glass bowl, electric mixer

Prep: 25 minutes   **Cook:** 45 minutes   **Cool:** 2½ hours

1/8th of pie: 187 calories, 3g fat, 176mg sodium, 39g carbs, 3.5g fiber, 20.5g sugars, 3g protein

Ingredients

Crust
1 cup Fiber One Original bran cereal
2 sheets (8 crackers) low-fat honey graham crackers, broken into pieces
3 tablespoons Splenda No Calorie Sweetener (granulated)
¼ cup light whipped butter or light buttery spread

Filling
⅓ cup fat-free liquid egg substitute
½ cup cornstarch
½ cup Splenda No Calorie Sweetener (granulated)
½ cup granulated white sugar
⅛ teaspoon salt
½ cup freshly squeezed lemon juice

Meringue
½ cup liquid egg whites (about 4 egg whites)
⅛ teaspoon cream of tartar
¼ cup Splenda No Calorie Sweetener (granulated)
¼ cup granulated white sugar
¼ teaspoon vanilla extract

For a pic of this recipe, see the first photo insert. Yay!

Directions

Preheat oven to 350 degrees. Spray a 9-inch pie pan with nonstick spray.

To make the crust, in a blender or food processor, grind cereal and graham cracker pieces into crumbs. Transfer to a medium bowl, and mix in Splenda.

Place butter in a small microwave-safe bowl. Add 2 tablespoons water, and microwave for 30 seconds, or until butter has melted. Add mixture to the medium bowl, and thoroughly mix.

Evenly distribute crust mixture along the bottom of the pie pan, and firmly press to form the crust. Press it into the edges and up along the sides of the pan.

Bake until firm, about 10 minutes. Remove pan, and reduce temperature to 325 degrees.

To make the filling, pour egg substitute into a medium-large bowl. In a small nonstick pot, combine cornstarch with 1½ cups cold water, and stir to dissolve. Add remaining filling ingredients *except* lemon juice.

Set heat to medium. Stirring frequently, cook until thickened to a gel-like consistency, about 15 minutes. Remove from heat.

Remove ½ cup of the thickened mixture from the pot. While whisking the egg substitute in the bowl, slowly add the ½ cup of thickened mixture to the bowl in spoonfuls.

Gently stir contents of the bowl into the mixture in the pot. Set heat to low. Cook and stir until well mixed and very thick, 1 to 2 minutes. Carefully add lemon juice and stir until just mixed. Transfer filling to the pie crust.

To make the meringue, quickly set out all measured ingredients. In a large metal or glass bowl, combine egg whites with cream of tartar. With an electric mixer set to high speed, beat until fluffy and slightly stiff, about 3 minutes.

Continue to beat while gradually adding Splenda, sugar, and vanilla extract. Beat until fully blended and stiff peaks form, 2 to 3 minutes.

Evenly spread meringue over the exposed filling without covering the edges of the pan. Bake until meringue is cooked through and lightly browned, 10 to 12 minutes.

Let cool and set completely, about 2½ hours. Enjoy!

MAKES 8 SERVINGS

187 calories per serving

Cheery Cherry Pie

You'll Need: 9-inch pie pan, nonstick spray, blender or food processor, medium bowl, small microwave-safe bowl, medium nonstick pot

Prep: 20 minutes   **Cook:** 30 minutes   **Cool:** 2 hours

1/8th of pie: 126 calories, 3g fat, 168mg sodium, 26g carbs, 5g fiber, 10.5g sugars, 1g protein

Ingredients

Crust
1 cup Fiber One Original bran cereal
2 sheets (8 crackers) low-fat honey
       graham crackers, broken into pieces
3 tablespoons Splenda No Calorie
       Sweetener (granulated)
¼ teaspoon cinnamon
¼ cup light whipped butter or light buttery spread

Sugar Alternative:

199 calories, 45g carbs,
31.5g sugars

Filling
3 tablespoons cornstarch
4 cups frozen unsweetened pitted dark sweet cherries
⅔ cup Splenda No Calorie Sweetener (granulated)
1 teaspoon lemon juice
¼ teaspoon cinnamon
¼ teaspoon salt

Optional topping: Fat Free Reddi-wip

Directions

Preheat oven to 350 degrees. Spray a 9-inch pie pan with nonstick spray.

To make the crust, in a blender or food processor, grind cereal and graham cracker pieces into crumbs. Transfer to a medium bowl, and mix in Splenda and cinnamon.

Place butter in a small microwave-safe bowl. Add 2 tablespoons water, and microwave for 30 seconds, or until butter has melted. Add mixture to the medium bowl, and thoroughly mix.

Evenly distribute crust mixture along the bottom of the pie pan, and firmly press to form the crust. Press it into the edges and up along the sides of the pan.

Bake until firm, about 10 minutes.

To make the filling, in a medium nonstick pot, combine cornstarch with ½ cup cold water, and stir to dissolve. Add remaining ingredients, and stir well.

Set heat to medium, and stirring frequently, cook until mixture has thickened, 16 to 18 minutes.

Carefully transfer filling to the pie pan.

Let cool and set completely, about 2 hours. Enjoy!

MAKES 8 SERVINGS

126 calories per serving

PB & Banana Cream Pie

You'll Need: medium nonstick pot, whisk, 9-inch pie pan

Prep: 15 minutes   **Cook:** 15 minutes   **Cool/Chill:** 1 hour and 45 minutes

1/8th of pie: 183 calories, 7g fat, 184mg sodium, 24.5g carbs, 1.5g fiber, 9.5g sugars, 5.5g protein

Ingredients

¼ cup cornstarch
2 cups light plain soymilk
½ cup Splenda No Calorie Sweetener (granulated)
¼ teaspoon salt
⅓ cup reduced-fat peanut butter
½ teaspoon vanilla extract
2 medium bananas
1 cup Cool Whip Free (thawed)
¼ cup peanut butter baking chips, chopped

Directions

In a medium nonstick pot, combine cornstarch with soymilk, and stir to dissolve. Add Splenda and salt, and mix well. Set heat to medium. Whisking constantly, cook until thickened, 12 to 14 minutes.

Remove from heat, and stir in peanut butter and vanilla extract until uniform.

Pour half of the mixture into a 9-inch pie pan, and smooth out the top.

Slice 1 banana into coins, and lay coins over the mixture in the pan.

Top with the remaining mixture, and smooth out the top.

Let set and cool completely, about 1 hour.

Refrigerate until chilled, at least 45 minutes.

Just before serving, spread pie with Cool Whip. Slice the remaining banana into coins, and lay over the Cool Whip. Sprinkle with chopped peanut butter chips, and devour!

MAKES 8 SERVINGS

183 calories per serving

✳ Flip to the photo inserts to see dozens of recipe pics! And for photos of ALL the recipes, go to **hungry-girl.com/books.**

Overnight Chocolate Layered Pie

You'll Need: 9-inch by 13-inch baking pan

Prep: 10 minutes   **Chill:** 6 hours

1/12th of pie: 131 calories, 3.5g fat, 170mg sodium, 24.5g carbs, 1g fiber, 8g sugars, 2g protein

Ingredients

12 sheets (48 crackers) low-fat honey graham crackers
4 sugar-free chocolate pudding snacks with 60 calories or less each
2 cups Cool Whip Free (thawed)
¼ cup mini semi-sweet chocolate chips

Directions

Place 6 graham cracker sheets in a single layer in a 9-inch by 13-inch baking pan. Gently spread 2 pudding snacks over the graham crackers.

Repeat layering with remaining graham crackers and pudding snacks.

Spread Cool Whip over the top pudding layer, and sprinkle with chocolate chips.

Refrigerate until graham crackers are soft, overnight or at least 6 hours. Enjoy!

MAKES 12 SERVINGS

Scoopy Chocolate Marshmallow Cream Pie

You'll Need: large bowl, whisk, 8-inch by 8-inch baking pan

Prep: 15 minutes   **Chill:** 1 hour

> **1/9th of pie (about 1/2 cup):** 130 calories, 2.5g fat, 199mg sodium, 24g carbs, 0.5g fiber, 11.5g sugars, 2.5g protein

Ingredients

1½ cups fat-free milk
One 4-serving box Jell-O Sugar Free Fat Free Chocolate Instant pudding mix
One 8-ounce container Cool Whip Free (thawed)
1 cup mini marshmallows
3 tablespoons mini semi-sweet chocolate chips
2 sheets (8 crackers) chocolate graham crackers, crushed

Directions

Pour milk into a large bowl. Add pudding mix and whisk until smooth and thickened, about 2 minutes. Fold in 1½ cups Cool Whip until uniform.

Spread mixture into an 8-inch by 8-inch baking pan.

Fold marshmallows and chocolate chips into the remaining Cool Whip. Spread mixture over the pudding mixture in the pan.

Cover and refrigerate until chilled and set, at least 1 hour.

Just before serving, sprinkle with crushed graham crackers. Dig in!

MAKES 9 SERVINGS

130 calories per serving

Scoopy Mocha-Coconut Cream Pie

You'll Need: glass, large bowl, whisk, 8-inch by 8-inch baking pan

Prep: 15 minutes   **Chill:** 1 hour

1/9th of pie (about 1/3 cup): 105 calories, 2.5g fat, 191mg sodium, 18g carbs, 1g fiber, 7g sugars, 2g protein

Ingredients

1 tablespoon instant coffee granules
1 teaspoon mini semi-sweet chocolate chips
1¼ cups fat-free milk
½ teaspoon coconut extract
One 4-serving box Jell-O Sugar Free Fat Free Chocolate Instant pudding mix
¼ cup plus 2 tablespoons shredded sweetened coconut
One 8-ounce container Cool Whip Free (thawed)
1 sheet (4 crackers) chocolate graham crackers, crushed

Directions

Place coffee granules and chocolate chips in a glass. Add ¼ cup very hot water, and stir until mostly dissolved.

Transfer mixture to a large bowl. Add milk, coconut extract, and pudding mix. Whisk until smooth and thickened, about 2 minutes.

Stir in ¼ cup shredded coconut. Fold in 1½ cups Cool Whip until uniform.

Spread mixture into an 8-inch by 8-inch baking pan.

Spread remaining Cool Whip over the pudding mixture in the pan.

Cover and refrigerate until chilled and set, at least 1 hour.

Just before serving, sprinkle with crushed graham crackers and remaining 2 tablespoons shredded coconut. Yum, yum, yum!

MAKES 9 SERVINGS

105 calories per serving

Coconut Cream Cutie Pies

You'll Need: 12-cup muffin pan, nonstick spray, large bowl, whisk, blender or food processor, medium bowl, small microwave-safe bowl, large plate, skillet (optional), small bowl (optional)

Prep: 25 minutes   **Cook:** 10 minutes, plus 5 minutes (optional)

Cool: 20 minutes, plus 15 minutes (optional)

1/12th of recipe (1 cutie pie): 117 calories, 4.5g fat, 226mg sodium, 20g carbs, 4.5g fiber, 5.5g sugars, 2g protein

Ingredients

Sugar Alternative:

131 calories, 23.5g carbs, 9.5g sugars

Filling
1 cup fat-free milk
¼ teaspoon coconut extract
One 4-serving box Jell-O Sugar Free
    Fat Free Vanilla Instant pudding mix
¼ cup shredded sweetened coconut
1 cup Cool Whip Free (thawed)

Crust
1½ cups Fiber One Original bran cereal
3 sheets (12 crackers) low-fat honey graham crackers, broken into pieces
¼ cup Splenda No Calorie Sweetener (granulated)
⅓ cup light whipped butter or light buttery spread

Topping
1 cup Cool Whip Free (thawed)
¼ cup shredded sweetened coconut

Directions

Preheat oven to 350 degrees. Spray a 12-cup muffin pan with nonstick spray.

To make the filling, pour milk into a large bowl. Add coconut extract and pudding mix, and whisk until smooth and thickened. Stir in shredded coconut. Fold in Cool Whip until uniform. Cover and refrigerate.

To make the crust, in a blender or food processor, grind cereal and graham cracker pieces into crumbs. Transfer to a medium bowl, and mix in Splenda.

Place butter in a small microwave-safe bowl. Add 3 tablespoons water, and microwave for 35 seconds, or until butter has melted. Add to the medium bowl, and thoroughly mix.

Evenly distribute crust mixture among the cups of the muffin pan. Firmly press mixture into the edges and up along the sides of each cup to form each mini crust. (Don't worry if it doesn't go all the way up the sides.)

Bake until firm, about 10 minutes. Let cool completely, about 20 minutes.

Gently remove crusts from the pan, and place on a large plate. Evenly distribute filling among the crusts, and smooth out with the back of a spoon.

Top pies with remaining 1 cup Cool Whip.

For a toasted coconut topping (optional), bring a skillet to medium heat. Cook and stir remaining ¼ cup shredded coconut until lightly browned, about 4 minutes. Transfer to a small bowl, and let cool completely, about 15 minutes.

Sprinkle pies with shredded coconut. Yum!

MAKES 12 SERVINGS

117 calories per serving

Banana Cream Cutie Pies

You'll Need: 12-cup muffin pan, nonstick spray, large bowl, whisk, blender or food processor, 2 medium bowls, small microwave-safe bowl, large plate

Prep: 30 minutes   **Cook:** 10 minutes   **Cool:** 20 minutes

1/12th of recipe (1 cutie pie): 108 calories, 3g fat, 207mg sodium, 21.5g carbs, 4g fiber, 6g sugars, 1.5g protein

Ingredients

Sugar Alternative:

122 calories, 25g carbs, 10g sugars

Filling
1 cup fat-free milk
¼ teaspoon vanilla extract
One 4-serving box Jell-O Sugar Free
      Fat Free Vanilla Instant pudding mix
⅔ cup Cool Whip Free (thawed)
1 large banana

Crust
1½ cups Fiber One Original bran cereal
3 sheets (12 crackers) low-fat honey graham crackers, broken into pieces
¼ cup Splenda No Calorie Sweetener (granulated)
⅓ cup light whipped butter or light buttery spread

Topping
1 large banana
1 cup Cool Whip Free (thawed)

For a pic of this recipe, see the first photo insert. Yay!

Directions

Preheat oven to 350 degrees. Spray a 12-cup muffin pan with nonstick spray.

To make the filling, pour milk into a large bowl. Add vanilla extract and pudding mix, and whisk until smooth and thickened. Fold in Cool Whip until uniform. Cover and refrigerate.

To make the crust, in a blender or food processor, grind cereal and graham cracker pieces into crumbs. Transfer to a medium bowl, and mix in Splenda.

Place butter in a small microwave-safe bowl. Add 3 tablespoons water, and microwave for 35 seconds, or until just melted. Add to the medium bowl, and mix thoroughly.

Evenly distribute crust mixture among the cups of the muffin pan. Firmly press mixture into the edges and up along the sides of each cup to form each mini crust. (Don't worry if it doesn't go all the way up the sides.)

Bake until firm, about 10 minutes. Let cool completely, about 20 minutes.

Meanwhile, in a medium bowl, mash one banana. Stir mashed banana into filling mixture.

Gently remove crusts from the pan, and place on a large plate. Evenly distribute filling among the crusts, and smooth out with the back of a spoon.

Slice the remaining banana into coins, and evenly place over the pies.

Top with Cool Whip, and eat up!

MAKES 12 SERVINGS

108 calories per serving

Streusel-Topped Pumpkin Cutie Pies

You'll Need: 12-cup muffin pan, foil baking cups, large bowl, whisk, medium bowl, large plate

Prep: 15 minutes   **Cook:** 35 minutes   **Cool/Chill:** 2 hours

1/12th of recipe (1 cutie pie): 145 calories, 3g fat, 91mg sodium, 25g carbs, 2g fiber, 19.5g sugars, 4.5g protein

Ingredients

No-Calorie Sweetener Alternative:

107 calories, 15g carbs, 8g sugars

Filling
One 15-ounce can pure pumpkin
One 12-ounce can fat-free evaporated milk
⅔ cup granulated white sugar
½ cup fat-free liquid egg substitute
2 teaspoons pumpkin pie spice

Streusel
¼ cup plus 2 tablespoons old-fashioned oats
¼ cup whole-wheat flour
¼ cup brown sugar (not packed)
¼ cup light whipped butter or light buttery spread
3 tablespoons chopped pecans
1½ teaspoons cinnamon

Optional topping: Fat Free Reddi-wip, cinnamon

Directions

Preheat oven to 350 degrees. Line a 12-cup muffin pan with foil baking cups.

In a large bowl, thoroughly whisk filling ingredients.

Evenly distribute filling among the cups of the muffin pan. (Cups will be very full!) Bake for 20 minutes.

Meanwhile, in a medium bowl, combine all streusel ingredients. Mash and stir until well mixed.

Evenly distribute streusel mixture among the baked filling in the cups. Bake until the edges of the filling are firm and golden brown, about 15 minutes.

Let cool completely, about 1½ hours. Gently remove pies from the pan, and place on a large plate.

Refrigerate until chilled, at least 30 minutes. Enjoy!

MAKES 12 SERVINGS

HG FYI:
These pies become sticky when they bake! A little mess never hurts anyone . . .

Hungry for More?

Have some more pie . . .

Fruity Pie:
* Ooey-Gooey Apple Pie Cones (page 265)
* Blueberry Pie Cones (page 268)
* Mini Dutch Apple Pies (page 288)
* Key Lime Pie-fait (page 306)
* Stuffed-Apple Apple Pie (page 318)
* DIY Apple Pie Nachos (page 342)

Pumpkin Pie:
* Streusel-Topped Pumpkin Pie in a Mug (page 26)
* Pumpkin Pie Cupcakes (page 50)
* Freezy Pumpkin Pie-wiches (page 197)
* Pumpkin Pie Crunchettes (page 252)
* Swirly Pumpkin Pie Cream Fluff Cups (page 276)
* Pumpkin Pie Pot Stickers (page 346)

And don't miss the freezy pies in Chapter 9 (page 208)!

CHAPTER 7

SOFTIES & WHOOPIE PIES

What's round, delicious, and low in fat and calories?
THESE RECIPES!

SOFTIES

For those of you who aren't in the know, softies are HG's version of big doughy cookies. They're like a cross between a soft cookie and a muffin top, and they ROCK. Enjoy this collection of softies . . .

Pumpkin Chocolate Chip Softies

You'll Need: baking sheet, nonstick spray, medium bowl, whisk

Prep: 10 minutes   **Cook:** 20 minutes

1/8th of recipe (1 softie): 131 calories, 3g fat, 100mg sodium, 23g carbs, 3.5g fiber, 9g sugars, 3g protein

Ingredients

1 cup canned pure pumpkin
¼ cup brown sugar (not packed)
2 tablespoons Splenda No Calorie Sweetener (granulated)
2 tablespoons light whipped butter or light buttery spread, room temperature
2 tablespoons fat-free liquid egg substitute
¼ teaspoon vanilla extract
¾ cup whole-wheat flour
1¼ teaspoons cinnamon
½ teaspoon baking powder
⅛ teaspoon salt
½ cup old-fashioned oats
3 tablespoons mini semi-sweet chocolate chips

Sugar Alternative:

140 calories, 25.5g carbs, 12g sugars

Directions

Preheat oven to 350 degrees. Spray a baking sheet with nonstick spray.

In a medium bowl, combine pumpkin, brown sugar, Splenda, butter, egg substitute, and vanilla extract. Whisk thoroughly.

Add flour, cinnamon, baking powder, and salt. Stir until smooth.

Stir in oats and chocolate chips. Spoon batter onto the sheet in 8 evenly spaced mounds. Use the back of a spoon to spread and flatten into 3-inch circles.

Bake until a toothpick inserted into the center of a softie comes out clean, about 20 minutes. Eat up!

MAKES 8 SERVINGS

Pretzel Chocolate Softies

You'll Need: baking sheet, nonstick spray, medium bowl, whisk, very small microwave-safe bowl

Prep: 10 minutes   **Cook:** 15 minutes

1/6th of recipe (1 softie): 135 calories, 3.5g fat, 197mg sodium, 22.5g carbs, 2g fiber, 10.5g sugars, 3g protein

Ingredients

¼ cup brown sugar (not packed)

2 tablespoons Splenda No Calorie Sweetener (granulated)

2 tablespoons light whipped butter or light buttery spread, room temperature

2 tablespoons no-sugar-added applesauce

2 tablespoons fat-free liquid egg substitute

¼ teaspoon vanilla extract

⅓ cup whole-wheat flour

2 packets hot cocoa mix with 20 to 25 calories each

¼ teaspoon baking powder

⅛ teaspoon salt

½ cup old-fashioned oats

½ ounce (about 24) thin salted pretzel sticks, broken into very small pieces

2 tablespoons mini semi-sweet chocolate chips

> **Sugar Alternative:**
>
> 148 calories, 26g carbs, 14.5g sugars

Directions

Preheat oven to 350 degrees. Spray a baking sheet with nonstick spray.

In a medium bowl, combine brown sugar, Splenda, butter, applesauce, egg substitute, and vanilla extract. Whisk thoroughly.

For a pic of this recipe, see the first photo insert. Yay!

Add flour, cocoa mix, baking powder, and salt. Stir until smooth.

Stir in oats. Spoon batter onto the sheet in 6 evenly spaced mounds. Use the back of a spoon to spread and flatten into 3-inch circles.

Sprinkle with pretzel pieces, and gently pat to adhere.

Bake until a toothpick inserted into the center of a softie comes out clean, about 10 minutes.

Place chocolate chips in a very small microwave-safe bowl. Microwave at 50 percent power for 1 minute. Stir and microwave at 50 percent power for 30 seconds; repeat, as needed, until melted.

Stir melted chocolate and drizzle over softies. Yum!

MAKES 6 SERVINGS

135 calories per serving

For more recipes, tips & tricks, sign up for FREE daily emails at **hungry-girl.com!**

PB Pretzel Softies

You'll Need: baking sheet, nonstick spray, medium bowl, whisk

Prep: 10 minutes   **Cook:** 10 minutes   **Cool:** 20 minutes

1/6th of recipe (1 softie): 169 calories, 6g fat, 212mg sodium, 23g carbs, 2g fiber, 7.5g sugars, 5g protein

Ingredients

¼ cup reduced-fat peanut butter
¼ cup brown sugar (not packed)
2 tablespoons Splenda No Calorie
    Sweetener (granulated)
2 tablespoons light whipped butter or light
    buttery spread, room temperature
2 tablespoons no-sugar-added applesauce
2 tablespoons fat-free liquid egg substitute
¼ teaspoon vanilla extract
⅓ cup whole-wheat flour
½ teaspoon baking powder
Dash salt
½ cup old-fashioned oats
½ ounce (about 24) thin salted pretzel sticks, broken into very small pieces

Sugar Alternative:

182 calories, 26.5g carbs, 11.5g sugars

Directions

Preheat oven to 350 degrees. Spray a baking sheet with nonstick spray.

In a medium bowl, combine peanut butter, brown sugar, Splenda, butter, applesauce, egg substitute, and vanilla extract. Whisk thoroughly.

Add flour, baking powder, and salt. Stir until smooth.

Stir in oats. Spoon batter onto the sheet in 6 evenly spaced mounds. Use the back of a spoon to spread and flatten into 3-inch circles.

Sprinkle with pretzel pieces, and gently pat to adhere.

Bake until a toothpick inserted into the center of a softie comes out clean, about 10 minutes.

Let cool completely, about 20 minutes. Enjoy!

MAKES 6 SERVINGS

169 calories per serving

PB&J Softies

You'll Need: baking sheet, nonstick spray, medium bowl, whisk

Prep: 15 minutes **Cook:** 10 minutes **Cool:** 20 minutes

1/6th of recipe (1 softie): 185 calories, 6.5g fat, 164mg sodium, 26g carbs, 2.5g fiber, 10g sugars, 5.5g protein

Ingredients

¼ cup reduced-fat peanut butter
¼ cup brown sugar (not packed)
2 tablespoons Splenda No Calorie Sweetener (granulated)
2 tablespoons light whipped butter or light buttery spread, room temperature
2 tablespoons no-sugar-added applesauce
2 tablespoons fat-free liquid egg substitute
¼ teaspoon vanilla extract
⅓ cup whole-wheat flour
½ teaspoon baking powder
Dash salt
¾ cup old-fashioned oats
3 tablespoons low-sugar strawberry preserves, room temperature

Sugar Alternative:

198 calories, 30g carbs, 14g sugars

Directions

Preheat oven to 350 degrees. Spray a baking sheet with nonstick spray.

In a medium bowl, combine peanut butter, brown sugar, Splenda, butter, applesauce, egg substitute, and vanilla extract. Whisk thoroughly.

Add flour, baking powder, and salt. Stir until smooth.

📷 For a pic of this recipe, see the first photo insert. Yay!

Stir in oats. Spoon batter onto the sheet in 6 evenly spaced mounds. Use the back of a spoon to spread and flatten into 2½-inch circles.

Form an indentation with the spoon in the center of each softie, large enough to hold ½ tablespoon preserves.

Bake until a toothpick inserted into the thickest part of a softie comes out clean, about 10 minutes.

Immediately fill the indentation in each softie with ½ tablespoon preserves. Let cool completely, about 20 minutes. Eat up!

MAKES 6 SERVINGS

185 calories per serving

For more recipes, tips & tricks, sign up for FREE daily emails at **hungry-girl.com!**

White Chocolate Macadamia Softies

You'll Need: baking sheet, nonstick spray, medium bowl, whisk

Prep: 10 minutes   **Cook:** 10 minutes

> **1/6th of recipe (1 softie):** 135 calories, 5g fat, 115mg sodium, 19.5g carbs, 1.5g fiber, 9g sugars, 2.5g protein

Ingredients

¼ cup brown sugar (not packed)
2 tablespoons Splenda No Calorie Sweetener (granulated)
2 tablespoons light whipped butter or light buttery spread, room temperature
2 tablespoons no-sugar-added applesauce
2 tablespoons fat-free liquid egg substitute
¼ teaspoon vanilla extract
⅓ cup whole-wheat flour
¼ teaspoon baking powder
⅛ teaspoon salt
½ cup old-fashioned oats
2 tablespoons white chocolate chips, chopped
2 tablespoons chopped macadamia nuts

Sugar Alternative:
148 calories, 23g carbs, 13g sugars

Directions

Preheat oven to 350 degrees. Spray a baking sheet with nonstick spray.

In a medium bowl, combine brown sugar, Splenda, butter, applesauce, egg substitute, and vanilla extract. Whisk thoroughly.

Add flour, baking powder, and salt. Stir until smooth.

Stir in oats and chopped white chocolate chips. Spoon batter onto the sheet in 6 evenly spaced mounds. Use the back of a spoon to spread and flatten into 3-inch circles.

Sprinkle with nuts, and gently pat to adhere.

Bake until a toothpick inserted into the center of a softie comes out clean, about 10 minutes. Enjoy!

MAKES 6 SERVINGS

135 calories per serving

Crazy for Coconut Softies

You'll Need: baking sheet, nonstick spray, medium bowl, whisk

Prep: 10 minutes   **Cook:** 10 minutes

1/6ᵗʰ of recipe (1 softie): 129 calories, 4g fat, 125mg sodium, 21g carbs, 2.5g fiber, 8.5g sugars, 3g protein

Ingredients

¼ cup brown sugar (not packed)
2 tablespoons light whipped butter or light buttery spread, room temperature
2 tablespoons no-sugar-added applesauce
2 tablespoons fat-free liquid egg substitute
¼ teaspoon coconut extract
⅓ cup whole-wheat flour
¼ teaspoon baking powder
⅛ teaspoon salt
¾ cup old-fashioned oats
¼ cup shredded sweetened coconut

Directions

Preheat oven to 350 degrees. Spray a baking sheet with nonstick spray.

In a medium bowl, combine brown sugar, butter, applesauce, egg substitute, and coconut extract. Whisk thoroughly.

Add flour, baking powder, and salt. Stir until smooth.

Stir in oats and shredded coconut. Spoon batter onto the sheet in 6 evenly spaced mounds. Use the back of a spoon to spread and flatten into 3-inch circles.

Bake until a toothpick inserted into the center of a softie comes out clean, about 10 minutes. Yum!

MAKES 6 SERVINGS

129

calories per serving

Banana Nut Softies

You'll Need: baking sheet, nonstick spray, medium bowl, whisk

Prep: 15 minutes   **Cook:** 15 minutes

> **1/6th of recipe (1 softie):** 149 calories, 4g fat, 110mg sodium, 25.5g carbs, 2.5g fiber, 10g sugars, 3.5g protein

Ingredients

¾ cup mashed ripe banana
¼ cup brown sugar (not packed)
2 tablespoons Splenda No Calorie
    Sweetener (granulated)
2 tablespoons light whipped butter or light
    buttery spread, room temperature
2 tablespoons fat-free liquid egg substitute
½ teaspoon vanilla extract
⅓ cup whole-wheat flour
¼ teaspoon baking powder
⅛ teaspoon cinnamon
⅛ teaspoon salt
¾ cup old-fashioned oats
2 tablespoons chopped walnuts

Sugar Alternative:

162 calories, 29g carbs, 14g sugars

Directions

Preheat oven to 350 degrees. Spray a baking sheet with nonstick spray.

In a medium bowl, combine banana, brown sugar, Splenda, butter, egg substitute, and vanilla extract. Whisk thoroughly.

Add flour, baking powder, cinnamon, and salt. Stir until uniform.

Stir in oats. Spoon batter onto the sheet in 6 evenly spaced mounds. Use the back of a spoon to spread and flatten into 3-inch circles.

Sprinkle with walnuts, and gently pat to adhere.

Bake until a toothpick inserted into the center of a softie comes out clean, about 12 minutes. Enjoy!

MAKES 6 SERVINGS

149 calories per serving

Caramel Apple Softies

You'll Need: baking sheet, nonstick spray, microwave-safe bowl, medium-large bowl, whisk

Prep: 15 minutes   **Cook:** 15 minutes

1/6ᵗʰ of recipe (1 softie): 142 calories, 3g fat, 125mg sodium, 25.5g carbs, 2g fiber, 11.5g sugars, 3g protein

Ingredients

4 cubes chewy caramel (like Kraft Traditional Caramels)
1 cup peeled and finely chopped Fuji apple
⅛ teaspoon cinnamon
¼ cup plus 1½ teaspoons brown sugar (not packed)
2 tablespoons Splenda No Calorie
    Sweetener (granulated)
2 tablespoons light whipped butter or light
    buttery spread, room temperature
2 tablespoons no-sugar-added applesauce
2 tablespoons fat-free liquid egg substitute
¼ teaspoon vanilla extract
⅓ cup whole-wheat flour
¼ teaspoon baking powder
⅛ teaspoon salt
¾ cup old-fashioned oats

Sugar Alternative:

155 calories, 29.5g carbs, 15.5g sugars

Directions

Preheat oven to 350 degrees. Spray a baking sheet with nonstick spray.

Vertically cut each caramel cube in half, and cut each half into 3 evenly sized pieces, for a total of 24 pieces.

In a microwave-safe bowl, sprinkle apple with cinnamon and 1½ teaspoons brown sugar, and stir to coat. Microwave for 2 minutes, or until slightly softened. Mix well.

In a medium-large bowl, combine Splenda with remaining ¼ cup brown sugar. Add butter, applesauce, egg substitute, and vanilla extract. Whisk thoroughly.

Add flour, baking powder, and salt. Stir until smooth.

Stir in apple mixture and oats. Spoon batter onto the sheet in 6 evenly spaced mounds. Use the back of a spoon to spread and flatten into 3-inch circles.

Place 4 caramel pieces on top of each softie, toward the centers.

Bake until a toothpick inserted into the center of a softie comes out clean, about 10 minutes.

Enjoy . . . They're best warm!

MAKES 6 SERVINGS

142 calories per serving

Vanilla-licious Oatmeal Softies

You'll Need: baking sheet, nonstick spray, medium bowl, whisk

Prep: 10 minutes   **Cook:** 10 minutes

1/6ᵗʰ of recipe (1 softie): 151 calories, 5g fat, 120mg sodium, 24g carbs, 2g fiber, 11g sugars, 3g protein

Ingredients

¼ cup brown sugar (not packed)

2 tablespoons Splenda No Calorie Sweetener (granulated)

2 tablespoons light whipped butter or light buttery spread, room temperature

2 tablespoons no-sugar-added applesauce

2 tablespoons fat-free liquid egg substitute

½ teaspoon vanilla extract

⅓ cup whole-wheat flour

1 tablespoon sugar-free French vanilla powdered creamer

¼ teaspoon baking powder

⅛ teaspoon salt

¾ cup old-fashioned oats

3 tablespoons white chocolate chips, roughly chopped

Sugar Alternative:

165 calories, 27.5g carbs, 15g sugars

Directions

Preheat oven to 350 degrees. Spray a baking sheet with nonstick spray.

In a medium bowl, combine brown sugar, Splenda, butter, applesauce, egg substitute, and vanilla extract. Whisk thoroughly.

Add flour, powdered creamer, baking powder, and salt. Stir until smooth.

Stir in oats and chopped white chocolate chips. Spoon batter onto the sheet in 6 evenly spaced mounds. Use the back of a spoon to spread and flatten into 3-inch circles.

Bake until a toothpick inserted into the center of a softie comes out clean, about 10 minutes. Mmmm!

MAKES 6 SERVINGS

151 calories per serving

WHOOPIE PIES

There's something completely magical about whoopie pies. Not exactly sure what that is, but they're as close to dessert perfection as possible. Portion-controlled, cream-filled, cakey . . . AHHHHHH!!!

VITATOPS 101:

What are they?

Vitalicious VitaTops are all-natural, vitamin-packed, low-fat, high-fiber muffin tops with 90 to 100 calories each. They come in a slew of varieties and are a must-have for HG whoopie pies!

Where are they sold?

Certain flavors—like the Deep Chocolate—can be found in many supermarket freezer cases. For the full flavor lineup, order them online at vitalicious.com. Not only are they great in these recipes, but they're also AMAZING as stand-alone sweets.

Freezy Cookies 'n Cream Whoopie Pie

You'll Need: small bowl, plate

Prep: 5 minutes   **Freeze:** 1 hour

Entire recipe: 164 calories, 3g fat, 200mg sodium, 38.5g carbs, 9.5g fiber, 15.5g sugars, 4.5g protein

Ingredients

1 Vitalicious Deep Chocolate VitaTop, partially thawed
¼ cup Cool Whip Free (thawed)
2 chocolate graham crackers (½ sheet), lightly crushed

Directions

Carefully slice VitaTop in half lengthwise (like you would a hamburger bun), so that you are left with 2 thin round "slices."

In a small bowl, fold crushed graham crackers into Cool Whip.

Spoon and spread Cool Whip mixture onto the bottom Vita slice. Top with the other slice to form a sandwich.

Place on a plate and freeze until filling is firm, about 1 hour. Enjoy!

MAKES 1 SERVING

Freezy Black Forest Whoopie Pie

You'll Need: small bowl, plate

Prep: 5 minutes   **Freeze:** 1½ hours

> **Entire recipe:** 157 calories, 2g fat, 150mg sodium, 38.5g carbs, 9.5g fiber, 18g sugars, 4g protein

Ingredients

1 Vitalicious Deep Chocolate VitaTop, partially thawed
¼ cup Cool Whip Free (thawed)
5 frozen unsweetened pitted dark sweet cherries, thawed, patted dry, halved

Directions

Carefully slice VitaTop in half lengthwise (like you would a hamburger bun), so that you are left with 2 thin round "slices."

In a small bowl, fold halved cherries into Cool Whip.

Spoon and spread Cool Whip mixture onto the bottom Vita slice. Top with the other slice to form a sandwich.

Place on a plate and freeze until filling is firm, about 1½ hours. Bite in!

MAKES 1 SERVING

Chill Out Choco-Coconut Whoopie Pie

You'll Need: small bowl, plate

Prep: 5 minutes   **Freeze:** 1 hour

Entire recipe: 169 calories, 5g fat, 170mg sodium, 35.5g carbs, 10g fiber, 16.5g sugars, 4.5g protein

Ingredients

1 Vitalicious Deep Chocolate VitaTop, partially thawed
3 tablespoons Cool Whip Free (thawed)
1 drop coconut extract
½ teaspoon mini semi-sweet chocolate chips
1 tablespoon shredded sweetened coconut

Directions

Carefully slice VitaTop in half lengthwise (like you would a hamburger bun), so that you are left with 2 thin round "slices."

In a small bowl, fold coconut extract into Cool Whip. Fold in chocolate chips and 2½ teaspoons shredded coconut.

Spoon and spread Cool Whip mixture onto the bottom Vita slice. Top with the other slice to form a sandwich.

Gently press remaining ½ teaspoon shredded coconut into the exposed Cool Whip mixture on the sides of the sandwich.

Place on a plate and freeze until filling is firm, about 1 hour. Enjoy!

MAKES 1 SERVING

169 calories per serving

Freezy-Cool Salted Caramel Whoopie Pie

You'll Need: plate

Prep: 5 minutes   **Freeze:** 1 hour

Entire recipe: 176 calories, 2.5g fat, 458mg sodium, 43.5g carbs, 9g fiber, 21g sugars, 4.5g protein

Ingredients

1 Vitalicious Deep Chocolate VitaTop, partially thawed
1 tablespoon fat-free, low-fat, or light caramel dip
3 tablespoons Cool Whip Free (thawed)
⅛ teaspoon coarse sea salt

Directions

Carefully slice VitaTop in half lengthwise (like you would a hamburger bun), so that you are left with 2 thin round "slices."

Drizzle ½ tablespoon caramel dip onto the bottom Vita slice. Spoon and spread Cool Whip over the caramel. Drizzle with remaining ½ tablespoon caramel dip.

Top with the other slice to form a sandwich. Place on a plate and freeze until filling is firm, about 1 hour.

Gently press sea salt into the exposed Cool Whip on the sides of the sandwich. Yum!

MAKES 1 SERVING

Too-Cool Mint Chocolate Whoopie Pies

You'll Need: medium bowl, plate

Prep: 5 minutes **Freeze:** 1 hour

> **¹/₂ of recipe (1 whoopie pie):** 153 calories, 3.5g fat, 150mg sodium, 35g carbs, 9g fiber, 15.5g sugars, 4g protein

Ingredients

2 Vitalicious Deep Chocolate VitaTops, partially thawed
½ cup Cool Whip Free (thawed)
1 drop green food coloring
1 drop peppermint extract
2 teaspoons mini semi-sweet chocolate chips

HG Alternative: Make these with Chocolate Mint VitaTops!

Directions

Carefully slice VitaTops in half lengthwise (like you would hamburger buns), so that you are left with 4 thin round "slices."

Place Cool Whip in a medium bowl. Fold in food coloring and peppermint extract. Fold in chocolate chips.

Spoon and spread Cool Whip mixture onto the 2 bottom Vita slices. Top with remaining slices to form 2 sandwiches.

Place on a plate and freeze until filling is firm, about 1 hour. So good!

MAKES 2 SERVINGS

For a pic of this recipe, see the first photo insert. Yay!

153 calories per serving

Mr. Puffy Pumpkinhead Freezy-Cool Whoopie Pie

You'll Need: small bowl, sealable plastic bag, scissors, plate

Prep: 10 minutes   **Freeze:** 1 hour

Entire recipe: 168 calories, 2.5g fat, 350mg sodium, 36g carbs, 10.5g fiber, 15g sugars, 8.5g protein

Ingredients

1 Vitalicious Deep Chocolate VitaTop, partially thawed
3 tablespoons Cool Whip Free (thawed)
2 tablespoons fat-free cream cheese, room temperature
2 tablespoons canned pure pumpkin
¼ teaspoon cinnamon
½ no-calorie sweetener packet

Directions

Carefully slice VitaTop in half lengthwise (like you would a hamburger bun), so that you are left with 2 thin round "slices."

In a small bowl, combine all other ingredients. Stir until smooth. Spoon mixture into a bottom corner of a sealable plastic bag. Remove air and seal. Snip off that corner with scissors, creating a small hole for piping.

Lay the bottom Vita slice flat, cut side down. Pipe some of the pumpkin mixture onto the Vita slice in the shape of a jack-o'-lantern face: 2 solid triangles for eyes and a squiggly mouth.

Lay the top Vita slice on a plate, cut side up. Evenly squeeze all of the remaining pumpkin mixture (there will be A LOT!) onto the Vita slice. Top with the bottom Vita slice, face side up.

Freeze until filling is firm, about 1 hour. Enjoy!

MAKES 1 SERVING

168 calories per serving

PB & Chocolate Chilly Whoopie Pie

You'll Need: small bowl, plate

Prep: 5 minutes   **Freeze:** 1 hour

> **Entire recipe:** 191 calories, 5.5g fat, 224mg sodium, 37.5g carbs, 10g fiber, 15g sugars, 8g protein

Ingredients

1 Vitalicious Deep Chocolate VitaTop, partially thawed
⅓ cup Cool Whip Free (thawed)
1 tablespoon powdered peanut butter
½ tablespoon chopped peanuts

Directions

Carefully slice VitaTop in half lengthwise (like you would a hamburger bun), so that you are left with 2 thin round "slices."

In a small bowl, stir powdered peanut butter into Cool Whip until uniform. Stir in peanuts.

Spoon and spread Cool Whip mixture onto the bottom Vita slice. Top with the other slice to form a sandwich.

Place on a plate and freeze until filling is firm, about 1 hour. Yum!

MAKES 1 SERVING

See page 8 for the powdered PB 411. And don't miss these other recipes featuring powdered PB: **PB Cheesecake Chocolate Cupcakes** (page 44) and **Freezy PB S'mores Sandwich** (page 200)!

191 calories per serving

Mini Red Velvet Cheesecake Whoopie Pies

You'll Need: 12-cup muffin pan, nonstick spray, medium bowl, glass, medium-large bowl, whisk, plate

Prep: 15 minutes   **Cook:** 10 minutes   **Cool:** 15 minutes

1/6th of recipe (1 mini whoopie pie): 108 calories, 2g fat, 282mg sodium, 19g carbs, 0.5g fiber, 11.5g sugars, 3g protein

Ingredients

¼ cup fat-free cream cheese
1 tablespoon powdered sugar
1 drop vanilla extract
¼ cup Cool Whip Free (thawed)
1 packet hot cocoa mix with 20 to 25 calories
1 tablespoon mini semi-sweet chocolate chips
Dash salt
1 teaspoon red food coloring
⅓ cup moist-style devil's food cake mix
⅓ cup moist-style yellow cake mix
2½ tablespoons fat-free liquid egg substitute

Directions

Preheat oven to 350 degrees. Spray a 12-cup muffin pan with nonstick spray.

In a medium bowl, combine cream cheese, powdered sugar, and vanilla extract. Stir until smooth. Add Cool Whip, and stir until uniform. Cover and refrigerate.

For a pic of this recipe, see the first photo insert. Yay!

Place cocoa mix, chocolate chips, and salt in a glass. Add ¼ cup very hot water, and stir until mostly dissolved. Add food coloring, and mix well.

In a medium-large bowl, combine cake mixes with egg substitute. Add cocoa mixture, and whisk until smooth.

Evenly distribute batter among the cups of the muffin pan, to form 12 mini pie halves. (Cups will be about ¼th of the way full.)

Bake until a toothpick inserted into the center of a pie half comes out clean, 6 to 8 minutes.

Let cool completely, about 15 minutes.

Plate six pie halves, flat sides up. Evenly distribute cream cheese mixture among the six pie halves.

Top each with one of the remaining pie halves, flat side down. Whoopie, you're done!

MAKES 6 SERVINGS

108 calories per serving

For more recipes, tips & tricks, sign up for FREE daily emails at **hungry-girl.com**!

CHAPTER 8

FREEZY DESSERT SANDWICHES

Not all cookbooks have a section of "freezy dessert sandwiches"—so let's take a moment to enjoy this special chapter, shall we? (Beat.) OK, time's up—start assembling!!!

Frozen Cannoli Sandwiches

You'll Need: medium-large bowl, plate

Prep: 15 minutes   **Chill/Freeze:** 1 hour and 45 minutes

1/8ᵗʰ of recipe (1 sandwich): 137 calories. 2.5g fat, 175mg sodium, 24g carbs, 1g fiber, 12.5g sugars, 4.5g protein

Ingredients

1 tablespoon Jell-O Sugar Free Fat Free Vanilla Instant pudding mix
1 cup fat-free ricotta cheese
⅔ cup Cool Whip Free (thawed)
2½ tablespoons granulated white sugar
1 tablespoon powdered sugar
⅛ teaspoon vanilla extract
2 tablespoons mini semi-sweet chocolate chips
8 sheets (32 crackers) cinnamon graham crackers, broken into 16 squares

No-Calorie Sweetener Alternative:

125 calories, 20.5g carbs, 8.5g sugars

Directions

Place pudding mix in a medium-large bowl. Add 2 tablespoons cold water, and vigorously stir until mostly smooth and slightly thickened.

Add ricotta cheese, Cool Whip, granulated sugar, powdered sugar, and vanilla extract. Stir until uniform.

Stir in chocolate chips. Cover and refrigerate until slightly thickened, about 15 minutes.

Lay 8 graham cracker squares on a plate, and evenly distribute ricotta mixture among them. Top each with another square.

Freeze until filling is firm, at least 1½ hours. Enjoy!

MAKES 8 SERVINGS

For a pic of this recipe, see the second photo insert. Yay!

Freezy Pumpkin Pie-wiches

You'll Need: medium bowl, plate

Prep: 10 minutes   **Freeze:** 1 hour

¼th of recipe (4 pie-wiches): 94 calories, 0.5g fat, 247mg sodium, 21g carbs, 0.5g fiber, 6.5g sugars, 1g protein

Ingredients

1 tablespoon Jell-O Sugar Free Fat Free Vanilla Instant pudding mix
½ cup Cool Whip Free (thawed)
¼ cup canned pure pumpkin
¼ teaspoon cinnamon
Dash pumpkin pie spice
32 caramel-flavored mini rice cakes

Directions

Place pudding mix in a medium bowl. Add 2 tablespoons cold water, and vigorously stir until mostly smooth and slightly thickened. Add Cool Whip, canned pumpkin, cinnamon, and pumpkin pie spice. Stir until uniform.

Lay 16 mini rice cakes on a plate, and evenly distribute pudding mixture among them. Gently top each with another mini rice cake.

Freeze until filling is firm, at least 1 hour. Yum!

MAKES 4 SERVINGS

The Triple-Chocolate Frost

You'll Need: small bowl, plate

Prep: 5 minutes   **Freeze:** 15 minutes

Entire recipe: 199 calories, 5g fat, 97mg sodium, 35.5g carbs, <0.5g fiber, 18g sugars, 3.5g protein

Ingredients

¼ cup light chocolate ice cream, slightly softened
1 teaspoon mini semi-sweet chocolate chips
2 full-sized chocolate-flavored rice cakes

Directions

In a small bowl, stir chocolate chips into slightly softened ice cream.

Spoon and spread ice cream mixture onto a rice cake. Gently top with the other rice cake.

Place on a plate, and freeze until ice cream is firm, at least 15 minutes. Enjoy!

MAKES 1 SERVING

Chocolate Banana Freezy Sandwiches

You'll Need: medium bowl, plate

Prep: 5 minutes   **Freeze:** 1 hour

> **1/4th of recipe (1 sandwich):** 90 calories, 2g fat, 100mg sodium, 17.5g carbs, 1g fiber, 6.5g sugars, 1g protein

Ingredients

½ cup Cool Whip Free (thawed)
2 tablespoons mashed ripe banana
4 sheets (16 crackers) chocolate graham crackers, broken into 8 squares

Directions

In a medium bowl, fold mashed banana into Cool Whip.

Lay 4 graham cracker squares on a plate, and evenly distribute Cool Whip mixture among them. Gently top each with another graham cracker square.

Freeze until filling is firm, at least 1 hour. Eat!

MAKES 4 SERVINGS

Freezy PB S'mores Sandwich

You'll Need: small bowl, plate

Prep: 5 minutes   **Freeze:** 1½ hours

> **Entire recipe:** 161 calories, 4.5g fat, 128mg sodium, 28.5g carbs, 1.5g fiber, 13g sugars, 3g protein

Ingredients

⅓ cup Cool Whip Free (thawed)
2 teaspoons powdered peanut butter
8 miniature marshmallows
1 teaspoon mini semi-sweet chocolate chips
1 sheet (4 crackers) chocolate graham crackers, broken into 2 squares

Directions

In a small bowl, stir powdered peanut butter into Cool Whip until uniform. Stir in marshmallows and chocolate chips.

On a plate, spoon and spread Cool Whip mixture onto a graham cracker square. Gently top with the other square.

Freeze until filling is firm, at least 1½ hours. Enjoy!

MAKES 1 SERVING

See page 8 for the powdered PB 411. And don't miss these other recipes featuring powdered PB: **PB Cheesecake Chocolate Cupcakes** (page 44) and **PB & Chocolate Chilly Whoopie Pie** (page 191)!

Freezy Pretzel'wich Minis

You'll Need: plate

Prep: 5 minutes   **Freeze:** 30 minutes

Entire recipe (5 sandwiches): 129 calories, 0.5g fat, 307mg sodium, 27g carbs, 1g fiber, 4g sugars, 2.5g protein

Ingredients

10 Snack Factory Original Pretzel Crisps
¼ cup Cool Whip Free (thawed)

Directions

Lay 5 pretzel crisps on a plate, and evenly distribute Cool Whip mixture among them.

Gently top each with another pretzel crisp. Freeze until Cool Whip is firm, at least 30 minutes. Tada!

MAKES 1 SERVING

Freezy PB Pretzel'wich Minis

You'll Need: small bowl, plate

Prep: 5 minutes   **Freeze:** 30 minutes

Entire recipe (5 sandwiches): 189 calories, 4.5g fat, 364mg sodium, 30g carbs, 1.5g fiber, 4.5g sugars, 5.5g protein

Ingredients

3 tablespoons Cool Whip Free (thawed)
2 teaspoons reduced-fat peanut butter
10 Snack Factory Original Pretzel Crisps

Directions

In a small bowl, stir Cool Whip with peanut butter until uniform.

Lay 5 pretzel crisps on a plate, and evenly distribute Cool Whip mixture among them. Top each with another pretzel crisp.

Freeze until filling is firm, at least 30 minutes. Enjoy!

MAKES 1 SERVING

📷 For a pic of this recipe, see the second photo insert. Yay!

Freezy Tart
Peach-Cobbler Squares

You'll Need: small blender or food processor, small bowl, plate

Prep: 5 minutes   **Freeze:** 1 hour and 20 minutes

1/2 of recipe (1 sandwich): 105 calories, 2g fat, 83mg sodium, 21g carbs, 1g fiber, 10g sugars, 1g protein

Ingredients

⅓ cup peach slices packed in juice (about 4 slices), drained and blotted dry
¼ cup Cool Whip Free (thawed)
¼ teaspoon cinnamon
1 no-calorie sweetener packet
2 sheets (8 crackers) cinnamon graham crackers, broken into 4 squares

Directions

In a small blender or food processor, combine drained peach slices, Cool Whip, cinnamon, and sweetener. Pulse until mostly smooth.

Transfer to a small bowl and freeze until slightly firm, about 20 minutes.

Lay 2 graham cracker squares on a plate. Lightly stir peach mixture, and evenly divide it between the squares. Gently top each with another graham cracker square.

Freeze until filling is firm, at least 1 hour. Yum!

MAKES 2 SERVINGS

105 calories per serving

Open-Faced PB-Caramel Bites

163 calories per serving

You'll Need: small bowl, plate

Prep: 5 minutes   **Freeze:** 30 minutes

> **Entire recipe (5 pieces):** 163 calories, 6.5g fat, 183mg sodium, 23.5g carbs, 1g fiber, 10g sugars, 3.5g protein

Ingredients

3 tablespoons Cool Whip Free (thawed)
2 teaspoons reduced-fat peanut butter
5 caramel-flavored mini rice cakes
1 ½ teaspoons mini semi-sweet chocolate chips

Directions

In a small bowl, stir Cool Whip with peanut butter until uniform.

Lay mini rice cakes on a plate, and evenly distribute Cool Whip mixture among them.

Sprinkle with chocolate chips. Freeze until Cool Whip mixture is firm, at least 30 minutes. Mmmm!

MAKES 1 SERVING

Freezy PB Sandwiches

You'll Need: plate

Prep: 5 minutes   **Freeze:** 1 hour

¹/₂ of recipe (1 sandwich): 145 calories, 5g fat, 156mg sodium, 22.5g carbs, 1g fiber, 6.5g sugars, 3g protein

Ingredients

2 sheets (8 crackers) low-fat honey graham crackers, broken into 4 squares
1 tablespoon reduced-fat peanut butter
½ cup Cool Whip Free (thawed)

Directions

Lay graham cracker squares on a plate, and spread with peanut butter.

Evenly divide Cool Whip between two of the squares. Gently top each with another graham cracker square, peanut butter side down.

Freeze until filling is firm, at least 1 hour. Enjoy!

MAKES 2 SERVINGS

145 calories per serving

Open-Faced Chocolate-Peanut Freezies

You'll Need: plate

Prep: 5 minutes   **Freeze:** 30 minutes

Entire recipe (6 pieces): 128 calories, 5.5g fat, 98mg sodium, 19g carbs, 1g fiber, 7g sugars, 2.5g protein

Ingredients

6 chocolate-flavored mini rice cakes
2 tablespoons Cool Whip Free (thawed)
2 teaspoons chopped peanuts
1 teaspoon mini semi-sweet chocolate chips

Directions

Lay mini rice cakes on a plate, and spread with Cool Whip. Sprinkle with peanuts and chocolate chips.

Freeze until Cool Whip is firm, at least 30 minutes. Yum!

MAKES 1 SERVING

Freezy Choco-Caramel Banana Bites

You'll Need: small bowl, plate

Prep: 5 minutes   **Freeze:** 30 minutes

1/2 of recipe (6 pieces): 103 calories, 0.5g fat, 158mg sodium, 24.5g carbs, 1g fiber, 11g sugars, 1g protein

Ingredients

¼ cup Cool Whip Free (thawed)
2 teaspoons light chocolate syrup
12 caramel-flavored mini rice cakes
½ large banana, sliced into 12 coins

Directions

In a small bowl, fold chocolate syrup into Cool Whip until uniform.

Lay mini rice cakes on a plate, and spread with Cool Whip mixture. Top each with a banana coin.

Freeze until Cool Whip mixture is firm, at least 30 minutes. Enjoy!

MAKES 2 SERVINGS

103 calories per serving

CHAPTER 9

ICE CREAM CUPCAKES & OTHER FROZEN TREATS

Ice cream cupcakes could very well be the CUTEST desserts of all time. But, as we all know, looks aren't everything, so it's great that they taste INCREDIBLE too. There are many other impressive frozen treats here as well. The recipes in this chapter aren't all made with actual ice cream—we've got a few swaps up our sleeve (shocking, we know!). And when you make these, people WILL "ooh" and "ahh" all over the place—just a heads-up!

Brownie Sundae Cupcakes

You'll Need: 12-cup muffin pan, nonstick spray, large bowl, platter (optional)

Prep: 20 minutes   **Cook:** 15 minutes   **Cool/Freeze:** 2 hours

> **1/12th of recipe (1 brownie sundae cupcake):** 136 calories, 2g fat, 214mg sodium, 28g carbs, 1.5g fiber, 15g sugars, 1.5g protein

Ingredients

1 ¾ cups moist-style devil's food cake mix
1 cup canned pure pumpkin
2 ¼ cups Cool Whip Free (thawed)
1 tablespoon light chocolate syrup
1 tablespoon rainbow sprinkles
12 maraschino cherries

Directions

Preheat oven to 400 degrees. Spray a 12-cup muffin pan with nonstick spray.

In a large bowl, mix cake mix with pumpkin until smooth and uniform. (Batter will be thick.) Evenly distribute batter among the cups of the muffin pan, and smooth out the tops.

Bake until a toothpick inserted into the center of a cupcake comes out clean, 10 to 12 minutes.

Let cool completely, about 30 minutes.

Turn a cupcake on its side, and slice in half vertically, so that you are left with a top and bottom half. Repeat with remaining cupcakes.

Place all of the bottom halves on a platter or in the muffin pan, cut sides up. Evenly distribute 1½ cups Cool Whip among them. Gently top with the other cupcake halves.

Freeze until firm, about 1½ hours.

Just before serving, top each cupcake with 1 tablespoon Cool Whip, ¼ teaspoon chocolate syrup, ¼ teaspoon sprinkles, and a maraschino cherry. Enjoy!

MAKES 12 SERVINGS

136
calories per serving

Mini Red Velvet
Ice Cream Cakes

You'll Need: 12-cup muffin pan, foil baking cups, glass, 2 large bowls, whisk, small bowl

Prep: 20 minutes   **Cook:** 20 minutes   **Cool/Freeze:** 2 hours

1/12th of recipe (1 mini cake): 117 calories, 2.5g fat, 198mg sodium, 21g carbs, 0.5g fiber, 11.5g sugars, 2g protein

Ingredients

1 packet hot cocoa mix with 20 to 25 calories
3 tablespoons mini semi-sweet chocolate chips
½ cup moist-style devil's food cake mix
½ cup moist-style yellow cake mix
¼ cup fat-free liquid egg substitute
½ tablespoon red food coloring
Dash salt
⅓ cup fat-free cream cheese
2 tablespoons powdered sugar
¼ teaspoon vanilla extract
One 8-ounce container Cool Whip Free (thawed)

Directions

Preheat oven to 350 degrees. Line a 12-cup muffin pan with foil baking cups.

Place cocoa mix and 1 tablespoon chocolate chips in a glass. Add ¼ cup very hot water, and stir until mostly dissolved. Add ⅓ cup cold water.

In a large bowl, combine cake mixes, egg substitute, food coloring, and salt. Add cocoa mixture, and whisk until smooth.

Evenly distribute batter among the cups of the muffin pan. (Cups will be about halfway full.)

Sprinkle with remaining 2 tablespoons chocolate chips. Bake until a toothpick inserted into the center of a cupcake comes out mostly clean, 16 to 18 minutes.

Let cool completely, about 30 minutes.

In a small bowl, combine cream cheese, powdered sugar, and vanilla extract. Stir until smooth.

Place Cool Whip in another large bowl, and fold in cream cheese mixture until uniform.

Evenly distribute Cool Whip mixture among the mini cakes. Freeze until Cool Whip mixture is firm, at least 1½ hours. EAT!

MAKES 12 SERVINGS

117 calories per serving

Freezy Vanilla Cupcakes

You'll Need: 12-cup muffin pan, foil baking cups, 2 large bowls, whisk

Prep: 15 minutes   **Cook:** 15 minutes   **Cool/Freeze:** 1½ hours

1/12th of recipe (1 cupcake): 98 calories, 1.5g fat, 129mg sodium, 20g carbs, <0.5g fiber, 10g sugars, 1g protein

Ingredients

1 cup moist-style yellow cake mix
¼ cup fat-free liquid egg substitute
¼ teaspoon baking powder
One 8-ounce container Cool Whip Free (thawed)
1 cup mini marshmallows

Directions

Preheat oven to 350 degrees. Line a 12-cup muffin pan with foil baking cups.

In a large bowl, combine cake mix, egg substitute, and baking powder. Add ⅓ cup water, and whisk until smooth.

Evenly distribute batter among the cups of the muffin pan. (Cups will be about halfway full.)

Bake until a toothpick inserted into the center of a cupcake comes out clean, 10 to 12 minutes.

Let cool completely, about 30 minutes.

In a large bowl, fold marshmallows into Cool Whip. Evenly distribute mixture among the cupcakes.

Freeze until Cool Whip mixture is firm, about 1 hour. Eat up!

MAKES 12 SERVINGS

For a pic of this recipe, see the second photo insert. Yay!

Freezy PB Pie Cups

You'll Need: 12-cup muffin pan, foil baking cups, large bowl, electric mixer

Prep: 15 minutes   **Freeze:** 3½ hours

> **1/12ᵗʰ of recipe (1 pie cup):** 134 calories, 6g fat, 132mg sodium, 16g carbs, 0.5g fiber, 8g sugars, 4g protein

Ingredients

½ cup reduced-fat creamy peanut butter
4 ounces (about ½ cup) fat-free cream cheese
¼ cup powdered sugar
½ cup light vanilla soymilk
One 8-ounce container Cool Whip Free (thawed)
3 tablespoons mini semi-sweet chocolate chips

Directions

Line a 12-cup muffin pan with foil baking cups.

In a large bowl, combine peanut butter with cream cheese. With an electric mixer set to medium speed, beat until uniform.

Reduce speed to low. Continue to beat while gradually adding powdered sugar, followed by soymilk. Beat until smooth, 2 to 3 minutes.

Fold in 1 cup Cool Whip until uniform. Evenly distribute mixture among the cups of the muffin pan.

Spread remaining Cool Whip over the mixture, and sprinkle with chocolate chips.

Freeze until firm, at least 3½ hours. Mmmm!

MAKES 12 SERVINGS

134 calories per serving

Freezy Downside-Up PB-Nana Dream Pie

You'll Need: large bowl, electric mixer, 9-inch pie pan

Prep: 15 minutes   **Freeze:** 4½ hours

1/8th of pie: 171 calories, 7g fat, 206mg sodium, 21g carbs, 1.5g fiber, 10g sugars, 6.5g protein

Ingredients

½ cup reduced-fat creamy peanut butter
4 ounces (about ½ cup) fat-free cream cheese
¼ cup powdered sugar
½ cup light vanilla soymilk
1 cup Cool Whip Free (thawed)
1 large ripe banana, thinly sliced into coins
2 sheets (8 crackers) cinnamon graham
    crackers, crushed

Optional topping: Fat Free Reddi-wip

HG Tip!
If frozen until solid, let pie sit at room temperature for 10 to 15 minutes before cutting and serving.

Directions

In a large bowl, combine peanut butter with cream cheese. With an electric mixer set to medium speed, beat until uniform.

Reduce speed to low. Continue to beat while gradually adding powdered sugar, followed by soymilk. Beat until smooth, 2 to 3 minutes.

Fold in Cool Whip until uniform. Fold in banana coins. Pour mixture into a 9-inch pie pan.

Top with crushed graham crackers. Cover and freeze until firm, at least 4½ hours. Enjoy!

MAKES 8 SERVINGS

Freezy PB&C Squares

You'll Need: large bowl, electric mixer, 8-inch by 8-inch baking pan

Prep: 15 minutes   **Freeze:** 3½ hours

¹/₉ᵗʰ of recipe: 146 calories, 6.5g fat, 195mg sodium, 17g carbs, 1g fiber, 8.5g sugars, 5.5g protein

Ingredients

½ cup reduced-fat creamy peanut butter
4 ounces (about ½ cup) fat-free cream cheese
¼ cup powdered sugar
½ cup light vanilla soymilk
1 cup Cool Whip Free (thawed)
2 sheets (8 crackers) chocolate graham crackers, crushed
2 tablespoons light chocolate syrup

Optional topping: Fat Free Reddi-wip

Directions

In a large bowl, combine peanut butter with cream cheese. With an electric mixer set to medium speed, beat until uniform.

Reduce speed to low. Continue to beat while gradually adding powdered sugar, followed by soymilk. Beat until smooth, 2 to 3 minutes.

Fold in Cool Whip until uniform. Pour mixture into an 8-inch by 8-inch baking pan.

Top with crushed graham crackers, and drizzle with chocolate syrup.

Cover and freeze until firm, at least 3½ hours. Devour!

MAKES 9 SERVINGS

146 calories per serving

Smothered PB&J Squares

You'll Need: large bowl, electric mixer, 8-inch by 8-inch baking pan, medium nonstick pot, medium bowl

Prep: 15 minutes   **Cook:** 15 minutes   **Freeze:** 3½ hours

1/9th of recipe (1 square with about 2 tablespoons topping):
152 calories, 6g fat, 184mg sodium, 19g carbs, 1.5g fiber, 10g sugars, 5.5g protein

Ingredients

No-Calorie Sweetener Alternative:

143 calories, 16.5g carbs, 7.5g sugars

½ cup reduced-fat creamy peanut butter
4 ounces (about ½ cup) fat-free cream cheese
¼ cup powdered sugar
½ cup light vanilla soymilk
1 cup Cool Whip Free (thawed)
1 tablespoon cornstarch
2 cups frozen unsweetened strawberries, partially thawed and sliced
2 tablespoons granulated white sugar
¼ teaspoon cinnamon
Dash salt

Directions

In a large bowl, combine peanut butter with cream cheese. With an electric mixer set to medium speed, beat until uniform.

Reduce speed to low. Continue to beat while gradually adding powdered sugar, followed by soymilk. Beat until smooth, 2 to 3 minutes.

Fold in Cool Whip until uniform. Pour mixture into an 8-inch by 8-inch baking pan.

Cover and freeze until firm, at least 3½ hours.

Meanwhile, in a medium nonstick pot, combine cornstarch with ½ cup cold water, and stir to dissolve. Add all remaining ingredients, and mix well. Set heat to medium. Stirring frequently, cook until thick and gooey, 12 to 14 minutes. Transfer to a medium bowl, and let cool completely. Cover and refrigerate.

Just before serving, top each portion with ⅑th of the strawberry mixture, about 2 tablespoons. Eat up!

MAKES 9 SERVINGS

HG FYI:
If you have leftovers, store the peanut butter squares in the freezer and the strawberry mixture in the fridge.

Brownie-Bottomed Ice Cream Cake

You'll Need: 8-inch by 8-inch baking pan, nonstick spray, large bowl

Prep: 10 minutes   **Cook:** 20 minutes   **Cool/Freeze:** 4½ hours

1/9th of cake: 186 calories, 3.5g fat, 285mg sodium, 37g carbs, 2g fiber, 18.5g sugars, 2g protein

Ingredients

1 ¾ cups moist-style devil's food cake mix
1 cup canned pure pumpkin
One 8-ounce container Cool Whip Free (thawed)
2 tablespoons rainbow sprinkles

Directions

Preheat oven to 400 degrees. Spray an 8-inch by 8-inch baking pan with nonstick spray.

In a large bowl, mix cake mix with pumpkin until smooth and uniform. (Batter will be thick.) Spread batter into the baking pan, and smooth out the top.

Bake until a toothpick inserted into the center comes out clean, 18 to 20 minutes.

Let cool completely, about 1½ hours.

Evenly top with Cool Whip and sprinkles. Freeze until Cool Whip is firm, at least 3 hours. Enjoy!

MAKES 9 SERVINGS

For a pic of this recipe, see the second photo insert. Yay!

Freezy Movie Concession Stand Pie

You'll Need: large bowl, 9-inch pie pan

Prep: 15 minutes   **Freeze:** 4 hours

1/8th of pie: 180 calories, 5g fat, 139mg sodium, 32g carbs, 0.5g fiber, 19.5g sugars, 2.5g protein

Ingredients

2 cups Cool Whip Free (thawed)
1 sugar-free vanilla pudding snack with 60 calories or less
15 caramel-flavored mini rice cakes, chopped
4 pieces Twizzlers Strawberry Twists, finely chopped
2 tablespoons mini semi-sweet chocolate chips
3 cups light vanilla ice cream, slightly softened
2 tablespoons light chocolate syrup
1 tablespoon chopped peanuts

Directions

In a large bowl, fold pudding into Cool Whip until uniform.

Fold in chopped rice cakes, chopped Twizzlers, and chocolate chips.

Spoon and spread slightly softened ice cream into a 9-inch pie pan. Spread Cool Whip mixture over the ice cream layer.

Drizzle with chocolate syrup, and sprinkle with peanuts.

Freeze until completely firm, at least 4 hours. Yum time!

MAKES 8 SERVINGS

For a pic of this recipe, see the second photo insert. Yay!

More movie-concession creations await—check out the **Movie Concession Stand Crunchers** (page 231) and **Movie Concession Cones** (page 263)!

Banana Split Pie

You'll Need: large bowl, 9-inch pie pan

Prep: 15 minutes   **Freeze:** 4 hours

1/8th of pie: 172 calories, 3.5g fat, 73mg sodium, 33g carbs, 2g fiber, 19.5g sugars, 3g protein

Ingredients

2 cups Cool Whip Free (thawed)
1 sugar-free chocolate pudding snack with 60 calories or less
3 cups light vanilla ice cream, slightly softened
1½ cups sliced strawberries
2 medium bananas, sliced into coins
2 tablespoons light chocolate syrup
1 tablespoon crushed peanuts
8 maraschino cherries

Directions

In a large bowl, fold pudding into Cool Whip until uniform.

Spoon and spread slightly softened ice cream into a 9-inch pie pan. Lay strawberry slices over the ice cream, and gently press to adhere.

Spread Cool Whip mixture over the layer of strawberry slices. Lay banana slices over the Cool Whip mixture, and drizzle with chocolate syrup.

Sprinkle with peanuts, and top with cherries. Freeze until completely firm, at least 4 hours. Yum!

MAKES 8 SERVINGS

Freezy Cookies 'n Cream Scoop Sundaes

You'll Need: plastic wrap, 1 medium bowl, 2 small bowls

Prep: 10 minutes   **Freeze:** 30 minutes

1/2 of recipe (1 sundae): 167 calories, 4g fat, 127mg sodium, 28.5g carbs, 0.5g fiber, 19.5g sugars, 3g protein

Ingredients

1 cup light vanilla ice cream
1 pack Nabisco 100 Cal Oreo Thin Crisps, crushed
¼ cup Fat Free Reddi-wip
2 teaspoons light chocolate syrup

HG Alternative: If you can't track down the cookies, use 1 ½ sheets (6 crackers) of chocolate graham crackers instead.

Directions

Place a ½-cup scoop of ice cream on a sheet of plastic wrap, and wrap it up completely. Use your hands to form the plastic-wrapped ice cream into a ball. Repeat with remaining ½ cup ice cream.

Freeze until firm, at least 30 minutes.

Place crushed cookies in a medium bowl.

Once firm, remove ice cream from the freezer and unwrap. One at a time, roll each ball in the crushed cookies until thoroughly coated.

Place each scoop in a small bowl, and top with 2 tablespoons Reddi-wip.

Drizzle with syrup, and sprinkle with any remaining crushed cookies. Mmmm!

MAKES 2 SERVINGS

167 calories per serving

Vanilla Sundae Scoops

You'll Need: plastic wrap, 1 medium bowl, 2 small bowls

Prep: 10 minutes   **Freeze:** 30 minutes

> **¹/₂ of recipe (1 sundae):** 167 calories, 4.5g fat, 89mg sodium, 28g carbs, <0.5g fiber, 20g sugars, 3g protein

Ingredients

1 cup light vanilla ice cream
6 Reduced Fat Nilla Wafers, crushed
¼ cup Fat Free Reddi-wip
1 teaspoon white chocolate chips, chopped

Directions

Place a ½-cup scoop of ice cream on a sheet of plastic wrap, and wrap it up completely. Use your hands to form the plastic-wrapped ice cream into a ball. Repeat with remaining ½ cup ice cream.

Freeze until firm, at least 30 minutes.

Place crushed wafers in a medium bowl.

Once firm, remove ice cream from the freezer and unwrap. One at a time, roll each ball in the crushed wafers until thoroughly coated.

Place each scoop in a small bowl, and top with 2 tablespoons Reddi-wip.

Sprinkle with chopped white chocolate chips and any remaining crushed wafers. Eat up!

MAKES 2 SERVINGS

Sweet 'n Salty Sundae Surprise

You'll Need: medium bowl

Prep: 5 minutes

Entire recipe: 190 calories, 4.5g fat, 201mg sodium, 32.5g carbs, 1g fiber, 20.5g sugars, 5.5g protein

Ingredients

½ cup fat-free vanilla ice cream
2 teaspoons fat-free, low-fat, or light caramel dip
1 tablespoon chopped salted peanuts
4 thin pretzel sticks, roughly crushed

Directions

Scoop ice cream into a medium bowl. Drizzle with caramel, and sprinkle with peanuts and crushed pretzel sticks. Then grab a spoon!

MAKES 1 SERVING

190

calories per serving

Very Vanilla Baked Alaska

You'll Need: large bowl (8-inch diameter at the top; capacity of at least 1½ quarts), plastic wrap, large bowl, 9-inch pie pan, baking sheet, large metal or glass bowl, electric mixer

Prep: 20 minutes   **Freeze:** 8 hours   **Cook:** 5 minutes

⅛ᵗʰ of recipe: 199 calories, 0.5g fat, 126mg sodium, 43g carbs, 0.5g fiber, 30.5g sugars, 5.5g protein

Ingredients

5 cups fat-free vanilla ice cream, slightly softened
1 cup mini marshmallows
16 Reduced Fat Nilla Wafers
½ cup liquid egg whites (about 4 egg whites)
⅛ teaspoon cream of tartar
¼ cup granulated white sugar
¼ cup Splenda No Calorie Sweetener (granulated)
¼ teaspoon vanilla extract

Directions

Begin with a large bowl with an 8-inch diameter at the top and a capacity of at least 1½ quarts. Line the bowl with plastic wrap, draping excess wrap over the sides.

In another large bowl, stir marshmallows into softened ice cream.

Evenly and firmly pack ice cream mixture into the large bowl lined with plastic wrap. Smooth out the top. Top with wafers, rounded sides down, in a single layer.

Cover with plastic wrap and freeze until completely firm, at least 8 hours.

Preheat oven to 500 degrees. Set out a 9-inch pie pan, a baking sheet, and all remaining measured ingredients.

To make the meringue, combine egg whites with cream of tartar in a large metal or glass bowl. With an electric mixer set to high speed, beat until fluffy and slightly stiff, about 3 minutes. Continue to beat while gradually adding sugar, Splenda, and vanilla extract. Beat until fully blended and stiff peaks form, 2 to 3 minutes.

Remove bowl from the freezer and uncover. Firmly place the pie pan over the bowl, upside down, and carefully flip so the pie pan is on the bottom. Gently tug on the plastic wrap to release the ice cream from the bowl, leaving the ice cream in the pie pan. Remove the plastic wrap.

Quickly and evenly spread meringue over the ice cream mound. Place pie pan on the baking sheet.

Bake until meringue is cooked through and lightly browned, about 3 minutes. Enjoy! (Freeze the leftovers and eat 'em frozen.)

MAKES 8 SERVINGS

199 calories per serving

* Flip to the photo inserts to see dozens of recipe pics! And for photos of ALL the recipes, go to **hungry-girl.com/books**.

CHAPTER 10

CRUNCHERS & CRUNCHETTES

Crunching is FUN. And there's something about munching on a dessert that has a crispy shell of some sort that just makes you feel satisfied. These desserts call for two MVPs in the HG kitchen—wonton wrappers and fillo shells. If you haven't used either, prepare to fall in love! And if these guys are staples in your house, you already know how much they rock. Let the crunching begin!!!

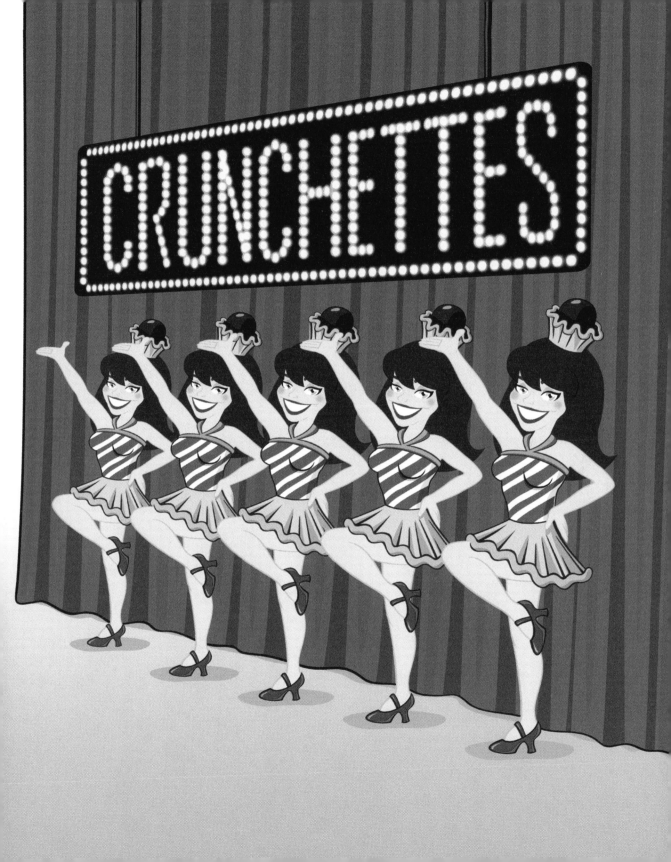

CRUNCHER TIPS 'N TRICKS

Find wonton wrappers in the refrigerated case at the supermarket, near the tofu. Don't confuse them with the larger egg roll wrappers!

To keep the crunchers nice and crispy, assemble them just before eating. If needed, store the filling in the fridge until you're ready to serve!

Nobody wants their food to stick, but if you overspray your muffin pan, the wonton wrappers may shrivel up on themselves. A light mist is all you need . . .

Have leftover wonton wrappers? Worry not! They can be frozen, but the entire stack needs to be fully thawed before you separate them—otherwise, they may tear. So before freezing, group 'em into 12-sheet stacks. This way you can easily thaw one stack whenever you're ready to make a Cruncher recipe! For best results, thaw them in the fridge.

Movie Concession Stand Crunchers

You'll Need: 12-cup muffin pan, nonstick spray, large bowl

Prep: 15 minutes   **Cook:** 10 minutes   **Cool:** 10 minutes

1/12th of recipe (1 cruncher): 83 calories, 2.5g fat, 83mg sodium, 13.5g carbs, 0.5g fiber, 5g sugars, 1g protein

Ingredients

1½ cups Cool Whip Free (thawed)
1 sugar-free vanilla pudding snack with 60 calories or less
4 pieces Twizzlers Strawberry Twists, chopped
3 tablespoons mini semi-sweet chocolate chips
3 tablespoons chopped peanuts
12 small square wonton wrappers

Directions

Preheat oven to 350 degrees. Spray a 12-cup muffin pan with nonstick spray.

In a large bowl, fold pudding into Cool Whip until uniform. Fold in chopped Twizzlers, chocolate chips, and peanuts. Cover and refrigerate.

Place each wonton wrapper into a cup of the muffin pan, and press it into the bottom and sides. Lightly spray with nonstick spray. Bake until lightly browned, about 8 minutes.

Let cool completely, about 10 minutes.

Evenly distribute Cool Whip mixture among the wonton cups. Enjoy!

MAKES 12 SERVINGS

83 calories per serving

Banana Split Crunchers

You'll Need: 12-cup muffin pan, nonstick spray, large bowl

Prep: 20 minutes   **Cook:** 10 minutes   **Cool:** 10 minutes

1/12th of recipe (1 cruncher): 85 calories, 2g fat, 66mg sodium, 15.5g carbs, 0.5g fiber, 6.5g sugars, 1g protein

Ingredients

1½ cups Cool Whip Free (thawed)
1 sugar-free vanilla pudding snack with 60 calories or less
1 cup finely chopped ripe banana
2 tablespoons chopped peanuts
2 tablespoons mini semi-sweet chocolate chips
12 small square wonton wrappers
2 tablespoons rainbow sprinkles
6 maraschino cherries, halved

Optional topping: Fat Free Reddi-wip

Directions

Preheat oven to 350 degrees. Spray a 12-cup muffin pan with nonstick spray.

In a large bowl, fold pudding into Cool Whip until uniform. Fold in banana, peanuts, and chocolate chips. Cover and refrigerate.

Place each wonton wrapper into a cup of the muffin pan, and press it into the bottom and sides. Lightly spray with nonstick spray. Bake until lightly browned, about 8 minutes.

Let cool completely, about 10 minutes.

Evenly distribute Cool Whip mixture among the wonton cups. Top with sprinkles.

Finish off each cup with a maraschino cherry half. Enjoy!

MAKES 12 SERVINGS

Snicker-ed Up Crunchers

You'll Need: 12-cup muffin pan, nonstick spray, large bowl

Prep: 15 minutes   **Cook:** 10 minutes   **Cool:** 10 minutes

1/12ᵗʰ of recipe (1 cruncher): 93 calories, 3g fat, 107mg sodium, 16g carbs, 0.5g fiber, 6.5g sugars, 1.5g protein

Ingredients

1 ½ cups Cool Whip Free (thawed)
1 sugar-free chocolate pudding snack with 60 calories or less
¼ cup finely chopped peanuts
2 tablespoons mini semi-sweet chocolate chips
12 small square wonton wrappers
⅓ cup fat-free, low-fat, or light caramel dip

Directions

Preheat oven to 350 degrees. Spray a 12-cup muffin pan with nonstick spray.

In a large bowl, fold pudding into Cool Whip until uniform. Fold in 3 tablespoons peanuts and 1 tablespoon chocolate chips. Cover and refrigerate.

Place each wonton wrapper into a cup of the muffin pan, and press it into the bottom and sides. Lightly spray with nonstick spray. Bake until lightly browned, about 8 minutes.

Let cool completely, about 10 minutes.

Gently swirl caramel dip into the Cool Whip mixture. Evenly distribute mixture among the wonton cups.

Sprinkle with remaining 1 tablespoon peanuts and 1 tablespoon chocolate chips. Eat up!

MAKES 12 SERVINGS

93 calories per serving

Cuckoo for Cannoli Crunchers

You'll Need: 12-cup muffin pan, nonstick spray, medium-large bowl

Prep: 15 minutes **Cook:** 10 minutes **Cool:** 10 minutes

1/12th of recipe (1 cruncher): 108 calories, 1.5g fat, 153mg sodium, 16g carbs, <0.5g fiber, 7.5g sugars, 5.5g protein

Ingredients

2 tablespoons Jell-O Sugar Free
    Fat Free Vanilla Instant pudding mix
2¼ cups fat-free ricotta cheese
2 cups Cool Whip Free (thawed)
¼ cup plus 1 tablespoon Splenda No
    Calorie Sweetener (granulated)
2 tablespoons powdered sugar
¼ cup mini semi-sweet chocolate chips
12 small square wonton wrappers

Sugar Alternative:

125 calories, 20.5g carbs, 12.5g sugars

Directions

Preheat oven to 350 degrees. Spray a 12-cup muffin pan with nonstick spray.

Place pudding mix in a medium-large bowl. Add ¼ cup cold water, and vigorously stir until mostly smooth and slightly thickened.

Add ricotta cheese, Cool Whip, Splenda, and powdered sugar. Stir until uniform.

Stir in chocolate chips. Cover and refrigerate.

Place a wonton wrapper in each cup of the muffin pan, and press it into the bottom and sides. Lightly spray with nonstick spray. Bake until lightly browned, about 8 minutes.

Let cool completely, about 10 minutes.

Evenly distribute pudding mixture among the wonton cups. Mmmm!

MAKES 12 SERVINGS

Can't find fat-free ricotta?

Grab light or low-fat—each has a reasonable 2.5g fat per ¼-cup serving. Part-skim is much heavier, with 4.5 to 6g fat per ¼ cup.

Piña Colada Crunchers

You'll Need: 12-cup muffin pan, nonstick spray, medium bowl, large bowl

Prep: 20 minutes   **Cook:** 10 minutes   **Cool:** 10 minutes

1/12ᵗʰ of recipe (1 cruncher): 88 calories, 1.5g fat, 249mg sodium, 15g carbs, 0.5g fiber, 5g sugars, 3g protein

Ingredients

One 8-ounce tub fat-free cream cheese

One 4-serving box Jell-O Sugar Free
    Fat Free Vanilla Instant pudding mix

¼ cup Splenda No Calorie
    Sweetener (granulated)

⅛ teaspoon coconut extract

2 cups Cool Whip Free (thawed)

One 8-ounce can crushed pineapple
    in juice, drained

12 small square wonton wrappers

¼ cup shredded sweetened coconut

Sugar Alternative:

102 calories, 19g carbs,
9.5g sugars

Directions

Preheat oven to 350 degrees. Spray a 12-cup muffin pan with nonstick spray.

In a medium bowl, stir cream cheese until smooth. In a large bowl, combine pudding mix with Splenda. Add coconut extract and ½ cup cold water, and vigorously stir until mostly smooth and slightly thickened. Add Cool Whip and cream cheese, and stir until uniform.

Stir in pineapple. Cover and refrigerate.

Place each wonton wrapper into a cup of the muffin pan, and press it into the bottom and sides. Lightly spray with nonstick spray. Bake until lightly browned, about 8 minutes.

Let cool completely, about 10 minutes.

Evenly distribute pudding mixture among the wonton cups, and sprinkle with shredded coconut. Yum!

MAKES 12 SERVINGS

88 calories per serving

Blueberry Cheesecake Crunchers

You'll Need: 12-cup muffin pan, nonstick spray, small nonstick pot, 3 medium bowls

Prep: 15 minutes   **Cook:** 25 minutes   **Cool:** 1 hour and 10 minutes

> **1/12th of recipe (1 cruncher):** 63 calories, 0.5g fat, 202mg sodium, 12g carbs, 0.5g fiber, 5g sugars, 2.5g protein

Ingredients

½ tablespoon cornstarch
1 cup frozen unsweetened blueberries
⅛ teaspoon cinnamon
Dash salt
3 tablespoons granulated white sugar
¾ cup fat-free cream cheese
2½ tablespoons Jell-O Sugar Free Fat Free Vanilla Instant pudding mix
¼ teaspoon vanilla extract
½ cup Cool Whip Free (thawed)
12 small square wonton wrappers

No-Calorie Sweetener Alternative:

53 calories, 9g carbs, 2g sugars

Directions

Preheat oven to 350 degrees. Spray a 12-cup muffin pan with nonstick spray.

In a small nonstick pot, combine cornstarch with ¼ cup cold water, and stir to dissolve. Add blueberries, cinnamon, salt, and 1 tablespoon sugar. Mix well.

Set heat to medium. Stirring frequently, cook until thick and gooey, 12 to 14 minutes.

📷 For a pic of this recipe, see the second photo insert. Yay!

Transfer to a medium bowl, and let cool completely, about 1 hour.

Meanwhile, in another medium bowl, stir cream cheese until smooth. In a third medium bowl, combine pudding mix with remaining 2 tablespoons sugar. Add vanilla extract and ¼ cup cold water, and vigorously stir until mostly smooth and slightly thickened. Add Cool Whip and cream cheese, and stir until uniform. Cover and refrigerate.

Place each wonton wrapper into a cup of the muffin pan, and press it into the bottom and sides. Lightly spray with nonstick spray. Bake until lightly browned, about 8 minutes.

Let cool completely, about 10 minutes.

Evenly distribute pudding mixture among the wonton cups, followed by blueberry mixture. Enjoy!

MAKES 12 SERVINGS

263 calories per serving

For more recipes, tips & tricks, sign up for FREE daily emails at **hungry-girl.com!**

Peaches & Cream Cheesecake Crunchers

You'll Need: 12-cup muffin pan, nonstick spray, small nonstick pot, 3 medium bowls

Prep: 15 minutes   **Cook:** 20 minutes   **Cool:** 55 minutes

1/12th of recipe (1 cruncher): 62 calories, 0.5g fat, 202mg sodium, 11.5g carbs, <0.5g fiber, 5g sugars, 2.5g protein

Ingredients

½ tablespoon cornstarch
1 cup frozen unsweetened sliced peaches, partially thawed and chopped
⅛ teaspoon cinnamon
Dash salt
3 tablespoons granulated white sugar
¾ cup fat-free cream cheese
2½ tablespoons Jell-O Sugar Free Fat Free Vanilla Instant pudding mix
¼ teaspoon vanilla extract
½ cup Cool Whip Free (thawed)
12 small square wonton wrappers

No-Calorie Sweetener Alternative:

52 calories, 9g carbs, 2g sugars

Directions

Preheat oven to 350 degrees. Spray a 12-cup muffin pan with nonstick spray.

In a small nonstick pot, combine cornstarch with ¼ cup cold water, and stir to dissolve. Add peaches, cinnamon, salt, and 1 tablespoon sugar. Mix well.

Set heat to medium. Stirring frequently, cook until thick and gooey, 8 to 10 minutes.

Transfer to a medium bowl, and let cool completely, about 45 minutes.

Meanwhile, in another medium bowl, stir cream cheese until smooth. In a third medium bowl, combine pudding mix with remaining 2 tablespoons sugar. Add vanilla extract and ¼ cup cold water, and vigorously stir until mostly smooth and slightly thickened. Add Cool Whip and cream cheese, and stir until mostly smooth and uniform. Cover and refrigerate.

Place each wonton wrapper into a cup of the muffin pan, and press it into the bottom and sides. Lightly spray with nonstick spray. Bake until lightly browned, about 8 minutes.

Let cool completely, about 10 minutes.

Evenly distribute pudding mixture among the wonton cups, followed by peach mixture. Yum!

MAKES 12 SERVINGS

Cherry Cream Crunchers

You'll Need: 12-cup muffin pan, nonstick spray, large bowl

Prep: 10 minutes   **Cook:** 10 minutes   **Cool:** 10 minutes

1/12th of recipe (1 cruncher): 58 calories, 0.5g fat, 40mg sodium, 12.5g carbs, 1g fiber, 6g sugars, 0.5g protein

58 calories per serving

Ingredients

12 small square wonton wrappers

3 cups frozen unsweetened pitted dark sweet cherries, thawed and drained

1½ cups Cool Whip Free (thawed)

HG Tip!
Got leftovers? Put 'em in the freezer! These pies taste fantastic frozen. (If frozen solid, just let them thaw for a couple of minutes.) Mmmm . . .

Directions

Preheat oven to 350 degrees. Spray a 12-cup muffin pan with nonstick spray.

Place each wonton wrapper in a cup of the muffin pan, and press it into the bottom and sides. Lightly spray with nonstick spray. Bake until lightly browned, about 8 minutes.

Let cool completely, about 10 minutes.

In a large bowl, gently mix cherries with Cool Whip. Evenly distribute cherry mixture among the wonton cups, and enjoy!

MAKES 12 SERVINGS

Fruit 'n Cream Crunchers

You'll Need: 12-cup muffin pan, nonstick spray, large bowl

Prep: 15 minutes   **Cook:** 10 minutes   **Cool:** 10 minutes

1/12th of recipe (1 cruncher): 50 calories, 0.5g fat, 52mg sodium, 10.5g carbs, 0.5g fiber, 3g sugars, 0.5g protein

Ingredients

1½ cups Cool Whip Free (thawed)
1 sugar-free vanilla pudding snack with 60 calories or less
12 small square wonton wrappers
½ cup chopped kiwi
½ cup grapes, halved
½ cup chopped strawberries

Directions

Preheat oven to 350 degrees. Spray a 12-cup muffin pan with nonstick spray.

In a large bowl, fold pudding into Cool Whip until uniform. Cover and refrigerate.

Place each wonton wrapper into a cup of the muffin pan, and press it into the bottom and sides. Lightly spray with nonstick spray. Bake until lightly browned, about 8 minutes.

Let cool completely, about 10 minutes.

Evenly distribute Cool Whip mixture among the wonton cups, followed by kiwi, halved grapes, and strawberries. Eat up!

MAKES 12 SERVINGS

50 calories per serving

German Chocolate Crunchers

You'll Need: 12-cup muffin pan, nonstick spray, medium bowl, large bowl

Prep: 20 minutes   **Cook:** 10 minutes   **Cool:** 10 minutes

1/12th of recipe (1 cruncher): 104 calories, 2.5g fat, 255mg sodium, 16.5g carbs, 1g fiber, 5g sugars, 3.5g protein

Ingredients

One 8-ounce tub fat-free cream cheese

One 4-serving box Jell-O Sugar Free
    Fat Free Chocolate Instant pudding mix

¼ cup Splenda No Calorie
    Sweetener (granulated)

½ teaspoon vanilla extract

2 cups Cool Whip Free (thawed)

12 small square wonton wrappers

2 tablespoons fat-free, low-fat, or light caramel dip

2 tablespoons finely chopped pecans

2 tablespoons mini semi-sweet chocolate chips

2 tablespoons shredded sweetened coconut

Sugar Alternative:

118 calories, 20g carbs, 9.5g sugars

Directions

Preheat oven to 350 degrees. Spray a 12-cup muffin pan with nonstick spray.

In a medium bowl, stir cream cheese until smooth. In a large bowl, combine pudding mix with Splenda. Add vanilla extract and ¾ cup cold water, and vigorously stir until uniform and slightly thickened. Add Cool Whip and cream cheese, and stir until uniform. Cover and refrigerate.

For a pic of this recipe, see the second photo insert. Yay!

Place each wonton wrapper into a cup of the muffin pan, and press it into the bottom and sides. Lightly spray with nonstick spray. Bake until lightly browned, about 8 minutes.

Let cool completely, about 10 minutes.

Evenly distribute pudding mixture among the wonton cups. Drizzle with caramel dip, and sprinkle with pecans, chocolate chips, and shredded coconut. Eat!

MAKES 12 SERVINGS

Hungry for More?

For more wonton-wrapper magic, don't miss the **Pumpkin Pie Pot Stickers** (page 346) and **Dreamy PB Chocolate Ravioli Puffs** (page 348)!

CRUNCHETTE FYI . . .

Find the mini fillo shells in the freezer aisle. They're generally located near the frozen fruit, pie crusts, and whipped topping.

S'mores Crunchettes

You'll Need: baking sheet

Prep: 5 minutes   **Cook:** 10 minutes

1/5th of recipe (3 crunchettes): 89 calories, 3.5g fat, 37mg sodium, 14.5g carbs, <0.5g fiber, 6g sugars, 1.5g protein

Ingredients

15 frozen mini fillo shells
2½ tablespoons mini semi-sweet chocolate chips
30 mini marshmallows
2 low-fat honey graham crackers (½ sheet), crushed

Directions

Preheat oven to 350 degrees.

Place shells on a baking sheet. Evenly distribute chocolate chips among the shells.

Bake until chocolate chips have softened, about 5 minutes.

Remove baking sheet, and preheat the broiler. Top each shell with 2 mini marshmallows.

Broil until marshmallows are puffy and golden brown, 1 to 2 minutes.

Sprinkle with crushed graham crackers, and enjoy!

MAKES 5 SERVINGS

PB&J Crunchettes

You'll Need: baking sheet, medium bowl

Prep: 10 minutes   **Cook:** 5 minutes   **Cool:** 5 minutes

1/5th of recipe (3 crunchettes): 140 calories, 6.5g fat, 96mg sodium, 17g carbs, 1g fiber, 4.5g sugars, 4.5g protein

Ingredients

15 frozen mini fillo shells
½ cup Cool Whip Free (thawed)
¼ cup reduced-fat peanut butter
2 tablespoons low-sugar strawberry preserves
¼ cup finely chopped strawberries

Directions

Preheat oven to 350 degrees.

Place shells on a baking sheet, and bake until lightly browned and crispy, 3 to 5 minutes.

Let cool completely, about 5 minutes.

In a medium bowl, mix Cool Whip with peanut butter until uniform.

Evenly distribute preserves among the shells, followed by Cool Whip mixture. Top with strawberries, and dig in!

MAKES 5 SERVINGS

Chocolate PB Crunchettes

You'll Need: baking sheet, medium bowl

Prep: 5 minutes   **Cook:** 5 minutes   **Cool:** 5 minutes

¹/₅ᵗʰ of recipe (3 crunchettes): 73 calories, 2.5g fat, 76mg sodium, 11g carbs, <0.5g fiber, 1g sugars, 2.5g protein

Ingredients

15 frozen mini fillo shells
1 sugar-free chocolate pudding snack with 60 calories or less
1 tablespoon reduced-fat peanut butter
½ cup plus 2 tablespoons Fat-Free Reddi-wip

Directions

Preheat oven to 350 degrees.

Place shells on a baking sheet, and bake until lightly browned and crispy, 3 to 5 minutes.

Let cool completely, about 5 minutes.

In a medium bowl, mix pudding with peanut butter until uniform. Evenly distribute among the shells.

Just before serving, top each shell with a 2-teaspoon squirt of Reddi-wip. Crunch away!

MAKES 5 SERVINGS

White Chocolate Raspberry Crunchettes

You'll Need: baking sheet

Prep: 5 minutes   **Cook:** 5 minutes

> **1/5th of recipe (3 crunchettes):** 86 calories, 3.5g fat, 33mg sodium, 12.5g carbs, 0.5g fiber, 5.5g sugars, 1.5g protein

Ingredients

15 frozen mini fillo shells
3 tablespoons white chocolate chips, chopped
15 raspberries

Directions

Preheat oven to 350 degrees.

Place shells on a baking sheet. Evenly distribute chopped white chocolate chips among the shells.

Bake until chocolate chips have softened, about 5 minutes.

Immediately press a raspberry into the center of each shell. Mmmm!!!

MAKES 5 SERVINGS

Over the Rainbow Crunchettes

You'll Need: baking sheet, medium bowl

Prep: 5 minutes   **Cook:** 5 minutes   **Cool:** 5 minutes

1/5th of recipe (3 crunchettes): 58 calories, 2g fat, 53mg sodium, 10g carbs, 0g fiber, 1g sugars, 1.5g protein

Ingredients

15 frozen mini fillo shells
1 sugar-free vanilla pudding snack with 60 calories or less
1½ teaspoons rainbow sprinkles
¼ cup plus 1 tablespoon Fat-Free Reddi-wip

Directions

Preheat oven to 350 degrees.

Place shells on a baking sheet, and bake until lightly browned and crispy, 3 to 5 minutes.

Let cool completely, about 5 minutes.

In a medium bowl, stir 1 teaspoon sprinkles into pudding. Evenly distribute among the shells.

Just before serving, top each shell with 1 teaspoon Reddi-wip. Sprinkle with remaining ½ teaspoon sprinkles, and enjoy!

MAKES 5 SERVINGS

For a pic of this recipe, see the second photo insert. Yay!

58 calories per serving

Pumpkin Pie Crunchettes

You'll Need: baking sheet, medium bowl

Prep: 5 minutes   **Cook:** 5 minutes   **Cool:** 5 minutes

> **1/5th of recipe (3 crunchettes):** 66 calories, 1.5g fat, 113mg sodium, 12g carbs, 1g fiber, 2g sugars, 2g protein

Ingredients

15 frozen mini fillo shells
½ cup canned pure pumpkin
1 sugar-free vanilla pudding snack with 60 calories or less
2 teaspoons brown sugar (not packed)
⅛ teaspoon pumpkin pie spice
⅛ teaspoon salt
¼ teaspoon cinnamon
¼ cup plus 1 tablespoon Fat-Free Reddi-wip

Directions

Preheat oven to 350 degrees.

Place shells on a baking sheet, and bake until lightly browned and crispy, 3 to 5 minutes.

Let cool completely, about 5 minutes.

In a medium bowl, combine canned pumpkin, pudding, brown sugar, pumpkin pie spice, and salt. Add ⅛ teaspoon cinnamon, and mix until uniform. Evenly distribute among the shells.

Just before serving, top each shell with a 1-teaspoon squirt of Reddi-wip. Sprinkle with remaining ⅛ teaspoon cinnamon, and dig in!

MAKES 5 SERVINGS

For a pic of this recipe, see the second photo insert. Yay!

Almond Kiss Crunchettes

You'll Need: baking sheet

Prep: 5 minutes   **Cook:** 5 minutes

1/5th of recipe (3 crunchettes): 128 calories, 7.5g fat, 45mg sodium, 16g carbs, 0.5g fiber, 8g sugars, 3g protein

Ingredients

15 frozen mini fillo shells
15 Hershey's Milk Chocolate Kisses
15 roasted almonds

Directions

Preheat oven to 350 degrees.

Place shells on a baking sheet. Place a Hershey's Kiss in each shell, flat side down.

Bake until Kisses are hot and have just softened, about 3 minutes.

Immediately press an almond into the center of each shell. Serve it up!

MAKES 5 SERVINGS

Coconut Cream Crunchettes

You'll Need: skillet, small bowl, baking sheet, medium bowl

Prep: 5 minutes   **Cook:** 10 minutes   **Cool:** 5 minutes

1/5th of recipe (3 crunchettes): 73 calories, 3g fat, 67mg sodium, 11.5g carbs, 0.5g fiber, 2g sugars, 1.5g protein

Ingredients

3 tablespoons shredded sweetened coconut
15 frozen mini fillo shells
1 sugar-free vanilla pudding snack with 60 calories or less
¼ cup plus 1 tablespoon Fat-Free Reddi-wip

Directions

Preheat oven to 350 degrees.

Bring a skillet to medium heat. Cook and stir shredded coconut until lightly browned, about 4 minutes. Transfer to a small bowl.

Place shells on a baking sheet, and bake until lightly browned and crispy, 3 to 5 minutes.

Let cool completely, about 5 minutes.

Place pudding in a medium bowl. Stir in two-thirds of the cooked shredded coconut. Evenly distribute among the shells.

Just before serving, top each shell with 1 teaspoon Reddi-wip. Sprinkle with remaining cooked shredded coconut, and enjoy!

MAKES 5 SERVINGS

CHAPTER 11

CRUNCHCAKES & DESSERT CONES

You've gotta chew the desserts in this chapter to believe 'em.
So creative and soooooo yummy! They're also kid favorites . . .
Just an added bonus. Enjoy!

TIPS 'N TRICKS FOR CRUNCHCAKES 'N CONES

To keep your goodies crunchy, assemble them just before eating. If needed, store the filling in the fridge until you're ready to serve!

Cake cones are the flat-bottomed, wafer-like cones—they have about 20 calories and less than half a gram of fat each. Sugar cones are the ones with pointy bottoms—each has about 50 calories and half a gram of fat. Both can usually be found just outside the ice cream aisle, in the snack aisle, or in the baking section!

Fruity Caramel Crunchcakes

You'll Need: medium bowl, plate

Prep: 5 minutes

Entire recipe: 180 calories, 2g fat, 229mg sodium, 39.5g carbs, 1g fiber, 21.5g sugars, 1.5g protein

Ingredients

¼ cup chopped strawberries
1 tablespoon low-sugar strawberry preserves
8 caramel-flavored mini rice cakes
2 teaspoons fat-free, low-fat, or light caramel dip
1 teaspoon mini semi-sweet chocolate chips
2 tablespoons Cool Whip Free (thawed)

Directions

In a medium bowl, combine strawberries with preserves, and stir to coat.

Lay rice cakes on a plate, drizzle with caramel dip, and top with strawberry mixture.

Sprinkle with chocolate chips, top with Cool Whip, and dive in!

MAKES 1 SERVING

180 calories per serving

Salted Caramel Gooey Apple Crunchcakes

You'll Need: 2 medium bowls, medium microwave-safe bowl

Prep: 10 minutes   **Cook:** 5 minutes

> **1/4th of recipe (1 crunchcake):** 127 calories, 1g fat, 354mg sodium, 27g carbs, 0.5g fiber, 11.5g sugars, 3g protein

Ingredients

¼ cup fat-free cream cheese
1 tablespoon Jell-O Sugar Free Fat Free Vanilla Instant pudding mix
1 no-calorie sweetener packet
⅛ teaspoon vanilla extract
½ cup Cool Whip Free (thawed)
1 cup thinly sliced Fuji apple
2 tablespoons fat-free, low-fat, or light caramel dip
4 full-sized caramel-flavored rice cakes
¼ teaspoon coarse sea salt

Directions

In a medium bowl, stir cream cheese until smooth. In another medium bowl, combine pudding mix with sweetener. Add vanilla extract and 2 tablespoons cold water, and vigorously stir until mostly smooth and slightly thickened. Add Cool Whip and cream cheese, and stir until uniform.

Place apple in a medium microwave-safe bowl. Cover and microwave for 3 minutes, or until softened. Blot away excess moisture. Add caramel dip, and stir to coat.

Spread pudding mixture onto the rice cakes. Evenly distribute the caramel-coated apples.

Sprinkle with salt, and dig in!

MAKES 4 SERVINGS

Pumpkin Cream 'n Caramel Crunchcakes

You'll Need: medium bowl, medium-large bowl

Prep: 10 minutes

> **¹/₆th of recipe (1 crunchcake):** 137 calories, 1g fat, 297mg sodium, 27.5g carbs, 0.5g fiber, 12g sugars, 3.5g protein

Ingredients

4 ounces (about ½ cup) fat-free cream cheese
2½ tablespoons Jell-O Sugar Free
        Fat Free Vanilla Instant pudding mix
2 tablespoons granulated white sugar
⅛ teaspoon cinnamon
Dash pumpkin pie spice
¼ teaspoon vanilla extract
1 cup Cool Whip Free (thawed)
⅓ cup canned pure pumpkin
6 full-sized caramel-flavored rice cakes
2 tablespoons fat-free, low-fat, or light caramel dip

No-Calorie Sweetener Alternative:

123 calories, 24.5g carbs, 8g sugars

Directions

In a medium bowl, stir cream cheese until smooth. In a medium-large bowl, combine pudding mix, sugar, cinnamon, and pumpkin pie spice. Add vanilla extract and ¼ cup cold water, and vigorously stir until mostly smooth and slightly thickened.

Add Cool Whip, pumpkin, and cream cheese, and stir until uniform.

Spread pudding mixture onto the rice cakes, and drizzle with caramel dip. Dig in!

MAKES 6 SERVINGS

137 calories per serving

Hideously Yummy Chocolate Caramel-PB Crunchcakes

You'll Need: medium bowl, large bowl, small bowl

Prep: 10 minutes

> **1/12ᵗʰ of recipe (1 crunchcake):** 135 calories, 2.5g fat, 295mg sodium, 23g carbs, 0.5g fiber, 6.5g sugars, 4.5g protein

Ingredients

One 8-ounce tub fat-free cream cheese
One 4-serving box Jell-O Sugar Free
    Fat Free Chocolate Instant pudding mix
¼ cup Splenda No Calorie Sweetener (granulated)
½ teaspoon vanilla extract
2 cups Cool Whip Free (thawed)
3 tablespoons creamy reduced-fat peanut butter
2 tablespoons fat-free, low-fat, or light caramel dip
2 tablespoons light vanilla soymilk
12 full-sized caramel-flavored rice cakes

Sugar Alternative:

149 calories, 26.5g carbs, 11g sugars

Directions

In a medium bowl, stir cream cheese until smooth. In a large bowl, combine pudding mix with Splenda. Add vanilla extract and ¾ cup cold water, and vigorously stir until uniform and slightly thickened. Add Cool Whip and cream cheese, and stir until uniform.

In a small bowl, vigorously stir peanut butter, caramel dip, and soymilk until uniform.

Spread pudding mixture onto the rice cakes, and drizzle with the peanut butter mixture. Eat!

MAKES 12 SERVINGS

Movie Concession Cones

You'll Need: medium bowl

Prep: 10 minutes

¹/₄ᵗʰ of recipe (1 cone): 129 calories, 4.5g fat, 100mg sodium, 21.5g carbs, 0.5g fiber, 7.5g sugars, 1g protein

Ingredients

1 cup Cool Whip Free (thawed)
1 sugar-free vanilla pudding snack with 60 calories or less
2 pieces Twizzlers Strawberry Twists, chopped
1 ½ tablespoons mini semi-sweet chocolate chips
1 ½ tablespoons chopped peanuts
4 cake cones

HG FYI:
These taste
GREAT frozen!

Directions

In a medium bowl, fold pudding into Cool Whip until uniform. Fold in chopped Twizzlers, chocolate chips, and peanuts.

Evenly distribute mixture among the cones. Eat up!

MAKES 4 SERVINGS

129 calories per serving

Turtle Cheesecake Cones

You'll Need: 2 medium bowls

Prep: 10 minutes

¹/₄ᵗʰ of recipe (1 cone): 174 calories, 3g fat, 508mg sodium, 30.5g carbs, <0.5g fiber, 17g sugars, 6.5g protein

Ingredients

¾ cup fat-free cream cheese

2½ tablespoons Jell-O Sugar Free
    Fat Free Vanilla Instant pudding mix

3 tablespoons granulated white sugar

¼ teaspoon vanilla extract

½ cup Cool Whip Free (thawed)

4 cake cones

2 tablespoons fat-free, low-fat, or light caramel dip

2 teaspoons mini semi-sweet chocolate chips

2 teaspoons finely chopped pecans

**No-Calorie
Sweetener Alternative:**

144 calories, 22.5g carbs,
8g sugars

Directions

In a medium bowl, stir cream cheese until smooth. In another medium bowl, combine pudding mix with sugar. Add vanilla extract and 2 tablespoons cold water, and vigorously stir until mostly smooth and slightly thickened. Add cream cheese and Cool Whip, and stir until uniform.

Evenly distribute pudding mixture among the cones. Drizzle with caramel dip, and sprinkle with chocolate chips and pecans. Mmmm!

MAKES 4 SERVINGS

Ooey-Gooey Apple Pie Cones

You'll Need: small nonstick pot, medium bowl

Prep: 10 minutes   **Cook:** 20 minutes   **Cool:** 1 hour

1/5th of recipe (1 cone): 84 calories, 0.5g fat, 67mg sodium, 19g carbs, 0.5g fiber, 10g sugars, 1g protein

Ingredients

1 teaspoon cornstarch
1½ cups peeled and chopped Fuji apples
1 tablespoon granulated white sugar
⅛ teaspoon vanilla extract
Dash salt
1 teaspoon cinnamon
5 sugar cones
½ cup plus 2 tablespoons Fat Free Reddi-wip

No-Calorie Sweetener Alternative:

76 calories, 17g carbs, 8g sugars

Directions

In a small nonstick pot, combine cornstarch with ¼ cup cold water, and stir to dissolve. Add apples, sugar, vanilla extract, and salt. Add ½ teaspoon cinnamon, and stir well.

Set heat to medium. Stirring frequently, cook until apples have slightly softened and mixture is thick and gooey, 14 to 16 minutes.

Transfer to a medium bowl, and let cool completely, about 1 hour.

Evenly distribute apple mixture among the cones.

Just before serving, top each cone with 2 tablespoons Reddi-wip. Sprinkle cones with remaining ½ teaspoon cinnamon. Yum!!!

MAKES 5 SERVINGS

 For a pic of this recipe, see the second photo insert. Yay!

Cookies 'n Cream Cones

You'll Need: medium bowl

Prep: 5 minutes

> **1/2 of recipe (1 cone):** 130 calories, 3g fat, 168mg sodium, 25.5g carbs, 0.5g fiber, 6g sugars, 1g protein

Ingredients

½ cup Cool Whip Free (thawed)
1 sugar-free vanilla pudding snack with 60 calories or less
1 pack Nabisco 100 Cal Oreo Thin Crisps, broken into small pieces
2 cake cones

Optional topping: Fat-Free Reddi-wip

HG Alternative: No Oreo Thin Crisps? Just use 1½ sheets (6 crackers) of chocolate graham crackers instead.

Directions

In a medium bowl, fold pudding into Cool Whip until uniform.

Fold in Oreo Thin Crisp pieces. Evenly divide mixture between the cones. Serve and enjoy!

MAKES 2 SERVINGS

Strawberry Shortcake Cones

You'll Need: large bowl

Prep: 15 minutes

1/12ᵗʰ of recipe (1 cone): 76 calories, 1g fat, 128mg sodium, 16g carbs, 0.5g fiber, 4g sugars, <0.5g protein

Ingredients

One 4-serving package Jell-O Sugar Free Fat Free Vanilla Instant pudding mix
One 8-ounce container Cool Whip Free (thawed)
1½ cups finely chopped strawberries
12 cake cones
1½ cups Fat Free Reddi-wip
3 Reduced Fat Nilla Wafers, crushed

Directions

Place pudding mix in a large bowl. Add ½ cup cold water, and vigorously stir until mostly smooth and slightly thickened. Add Cool Whip, and stir until uniform.

Stir in strawberries. Evenly distribute mixture among the cones.

Just before serving, top each cone with 2 tablespoons Reddi-wip. Sprinkle with crushed wafers, and enjoy!

MAKES 12 SERVINGS

Blueberry Pie Cones

You'll Need: small nonstick pot, medium bowl

Prep: 5 minutes   **Cook:** 20 minutes   **Cool:** 1 hour

Ingredients

1 teaspoon cornstarch
1½ cups frozen blueberries, thawed and drained
1 tablespoon granulated white sugar
⅛ teaspoon vanilla extract
Dash salt
1 teaspoon cinnamon
5 sugar cones
½ cup plus 2 tablespoons Fat Free Reddi-wip

No-Calorie Sweetener Alternative:

83 calories, 18.5g carbs, 8g sugars

Directions

In a small nonstick pot, combine cornstarch with ¼ cup cold water, and stir to dissolve. Add blueberries, sugar, vanilla extract, and salt. Add ½ teaspoon cinnamon, and stir well.

Set heat to medium. Stirring frequently, cook until mixture is thick and gooey, 16 to 18 minutes.

Transfer to a medium bowl, and let cool completely, about 1 hour.

Evenly distribute blueberry mixture among the cones.

Just before serving, top each cone with 2 tablespoons Reddi-wip. Sprinkle cones with remaining ½ teaspoon cinnamon. Mmmm!

MAKES 5 SERVINGS

91 calories per serving

CHAPTER 12

CREAM FLUFF CUPS, CREAM FLUFF STACKS & MORE DOUGH-BOTTOMED DESSERTS

Just dough it! Dough the right thing! Dough re mi! OK, enough of that . . . Each recipe in this chapter features some combination of refrigerated dough, creamy fillings, fruit, and sweet toppings. You'll FLIP over 'em . . .

JUST DOUGH IT:
TIPS FOR WORKING WITH REFRIGERATED DOUGH

Pizza cutters are GREAT for cutting the uncooked dough.

Grocery store out of Pillsbury Crescent Recipe Creations Seamless Dough Sheets? Grab a tube of Pillsbury Reduced Fat Crescent roll dough—it's virtually the same. The only differences are the perforations (just pinch to seal) and the listed serving size.

CREAM FLUFF CUPS

Cream Fluff Cups. They're like cream puffs . . . only different!

Mochaccino Cream Fluff Cups

You'll Need: 12-cup muffin pan, nonstick spray, glass, medium-large bowl, whisk, rolling pin (optional)

Prep: 15 minutes   **Cook:** 15 minutes   **Cool:** 15 minutes

1/12th of recipe (1 cream fluff cup): 89 calories, 3g fat, 220mg sodium, 13g carbs, 0.5g fiber, 3.5g sugars, 1.5g protein

Ingredients

1 teaspoon instant coffee granules
1½ tablespoons mini semi-sweet chocolate chips
½ cup fat-free milk
3 tablespoons Jell-O Sugar Free Fat Free Chocolate Instant pudding mix
1 cup Cool Whip Free (thawed)
1 package refrigerated Pillsbury Crescent Recipe
    Creations Seamless Dough Sheet

Directions

Preheat oven to 350 degrees. Spray a 12-cup muffin pan with nonstick spray.

Place coffee granules and ½ tablespoon chocolate chips in a glass. Add ¼ cup very hot water, and stir until mostly dissolved.

Pour coffee mixture and milk into a medium-large bowl. Add pudding mix and whisk until smooth and thickened, about 2 minutes. Fold in Cool Whip until uniform. Cover and refrigerate.

Roll or stretch out dough into a large rectangle of even thickness, at least 12 inches by 9 inches. Evenly cut dough into 12 squares. Place each square in a muffin cup, and press it into the bottom and up along the sides.

Bake until golden brown, 10 to 12 minutes.

Let cool completely, about 15 minutes.

Evenly distribute pudding mixture among the dough cups. Sprinkle with remaining tablespoon chocolate chips. Enjoy!

MAKES 12 SERVINGS

89 calories per serving

Swirly Pumpkin Pie Cream Fluff Cups

You'll Need: 12-cup muffin pan, nonstick spray, 2 medium bowls, large bowl, rolling pin (optional)

Prep: 15 minutes   **Cook:** 15 minutes   **Cool:** 15 minutes

> **¹/₁₂ᵗʰ of recipe (1 cream fluff cup):** 110 calories, 3g fat, 382mg sodium, 16.5g carbs, 0.5g fiber, 4g sugars, 3.5g protein

Ingredients

One 8-ounce tub fat-free cream cheese
One 4-serving box Jell-O Sugar Free Fat Free Vanilla Instant pudding mix
½ teaspoon vanilla extract
2 cups Cool Whip Free (thawed)
½ cup canned pure pumpkin
2 tablespoons sugar-free pancake syrup
½ teaspoon cinnamon
1 package refrigerated Pillsbury Crescent Recipe
    Creations Seamless Dough Sheet

Directions

Preheat oven to 350 degrees. Spray a 12-cup muffin pan with nonstick spray.

In a medium bowl, stir cream cheese until smooth. Place pudding mix in a large bowl. Add vanilla extract and ½ cup cold water, and vigorously stir until mostly smooth and slightly thickened. Add Cool Whip and cream cheese, and stir until uniform. Cover and refrigerate.

In another medium bowl, combine pumpkin, pancake syrup, and cinnamon, and stir until uniform. Cover and refrigerate.

Roll or stretch out dough into a large rectangle of even thickness, at least 12 inches by 9 inches. Evenly cut dough into 12 squares. Place each square in a muffin cup, and press it into the bottom and up along the sides.

Bake until golden brown, 10 to 12 minutes.

Let cool completely, about 15 minutes.

Gently swirl pumpkin mixture into the pudding mixture.

Evenly distribute mixture among the dough cups. Yum time!

MAKES 12 SERVINGS

110 calories per serving

For more recipes, tips & tricks, sign up for FREE daily emails at **hungry-girl.com**!

Vanilla Cream Fluff Cups

1/12th of recipe (1 cream fluff cup): 119 calories, 4g fat, 229mg sodium, 18.5g carbs, <0.5g fiber, 7g sugars, 1g protein

Ingredients

3 tablespoons Jell-O Sugar Free Fat Free Vanilla Instant pudding mix
2 cups Cool Whip Free (thawed)
1 package refrigerated Pillsbury Crescent Recipe Creations Seamless Dough Sheet
2 tablespoons fat-free, low-fat, or light caramel dip
¼ cup white chocolate chips, chopped

Directions

Preheat oven to 350 degrees. Spray a 12-cup muffin pan with nonstick spray.

Place pudding mix in a large bowl. Add ⅓ cup water, and vigorously stir until mostly smooth and slightly thickened. Add Cool Whip, and stir until uniform. Cover and refrigerate.

Roll or stretch out dough into a large rectangle of even thickness, at least 12 inches by 9 inches. Evenly cut dough into 12 squares. Place each square in a muffin cup, and press it into the bottom and up along the sides.

Bake until golden brown, 10 to 12 minutes.

Let cool completely, about 15 minutes.

Evenly distribute pudding mixture among the dough cups. Drizzle with caramel dip, and sprinkle with chopped white chocolate chips. Dig in!

MAKES 12 SERVINGS

119 calories per serving

Strawberry Shortcake Cream Fluff Cups

You'll Need: 12-cup muffin pan, nonstick spray, rolling pin (optional), medium-large bowl, medium bowl

Prep: 20 minutes   **Cook:** 15 minutes   **Cool:** 15 minutes

> **1/12th of recipe (1 cream fluff cup):** 95 calories, 3g fat, 157mg sodium, 15.5g carbs, 0.5g fiber, 5.5g sugars, 1g protein

Ingredients

1 package refrigerated Pillsbury Crescent Recipe Creations Seamless Dough Sheet
2 cups Cool Whip Free (thawed)
1 cup chopped strawberries
⅓ cup low-sugar strawberry preserves

Directions

Preheat oven to 350 degrees. Spray a 12-cup muffin pan with nonstick spray.

Roll or stretch out dough into a large rectangle of even thickness, at least 12 inches by 9 inches. Evenly cut dough into 12 squares. Place each square in a muffin cup, and press it into the bottom and up along the sides.

Bake until golden brown, 10 to 12 minutes.

Let cool completely, about 15 minutes.

In a medium-large bowl, fold strawberries into Cool Whip. Evenly distribute mixture among the dough cups.

In a medium bowl, thoroughly mix preserves with 2 teaspoons water.

Drizzle preserves mixture over Cool Whip mixture, and enjoy!

MAKES 12 SERVINGS

Banana Cream Fluff Cups

You'll Need: 12-cup muffin pan, nonstick spray, 2 medium bowls, small nonstick pot, rolling pin (optional)

Prep: 20 minutes   **Cook:** 25 minutes   **Cool:** 1 hour

> **1/12th of recipe (1 cream fluff cup):** 95 calories, 3g fat, 175mg sodium, 15.5g carbs, 0.5g fiber, 5.5g sugars, 1.5g protein

Ingredients

1 large ripe banana
½ cup light plain soymilk
1 tablespoon cornstarch
2 tablespoons granulated white sugar
Dash salt
1 teaspoon light whipped butter or light
    buttery spread
¼ teaspoon vanilla extract
1 package refrigerated Pillsbury Crescent Recipe
    Creations Seamless Dough Sheet
1 cup Cool Whip Free (thawed)

> **No-Calorie Sweetener Alternative:**
>
> 89 calories, 13.5g carbs, 3.5g sugars

Directions

Preheat oven to 350 degrees. Spray a 12-cup muffin pan with nonstick spray.

In a medium bowl, mash ¼th of the banana. Refrigerate the remaining ¾ths of the banana.

In a small nonstick pot, combine soymilk with cornstarch, and stir to dissolve. Stir in sugar and salt.

Set heat to medium. Stirring frequently, cook until thickened, 8 to 10 minutes.

Remove from heat, and stir in mashed banana, butter, and vanilla extract.

Transfer to a medium bowl, and let cool completely, about 45 minutes.

Meanwhile, roll or stretch out dough into a large rectangle of even thickness, at least 12 inches by 9 inches. Evenly cut dough into 12 squares. Place each square in a muffin cup, and press it into the bottom and up along the sides.

Bake until golden brown, 10 to 12 minutes.

Let cool completely, about 15 minutes.

Stir creamy banana mixture, and evenly distribute it among the dough cups. Evenly top with Cool Whip.

Slice remaining ¾ths of the banana into 12 coins, and place a banana coin over each dough cup. Enjoy!

MAKES 12 SERVINGS

 calories per serving

Caramel Apple Cream Fluff Cups

You'll Need: 12-cup muffin pan, nonstick spray, medium nonstick pot, medium bowl, rolling pin (optional), large bowl

Prep: 25 minutes   **Cook:** 25 minutes   **Cool:** 1 hour and 15 minutes

1/12th of recipe (1 cream fluff cup): 96 calories, 3g fat, 178mg sodium, 16.5g carbs, <0.5g fat, 6.5g sugars, 1g protein

Ingredients

1 teaspoon cornstarch
1½ cups peeled and finely chopped Fuji apples
1 tablespoon granulated white sugar
½ teaspoon cinnamon
⅛ teaspoon vanilla extract
Dash salt
1 package refrigerated Pillsbury Crescent Recipe Creations Seamless Dough Sheet
1½ cups Cool Whip Free (thawed)
2 tablespoons fat-free, low-fat, or light caramel dip

No-Calorie Sweetener Alternative:

93 calories, 15.5g carbs, 5.5g sugars

Directions

Preheat oven to 350 degrees. Spray a 12-cup muffin pan with nonstick spray.

In a medium nonstick pot, combine cornstarch with ⅓ cup cold water, and stir to dissolve. Add apples, sugar, cinnamon, vanilla extract, and salt. Stir well.

Set heat to medium. Stirring frequently, cook until apples have softened and mixture is thick and gooey, 8 to 10 minutes.

Transfer to a medium bowl, and let cool completely, about 1 hour.

Meanwhile, roll or stretch out dough into a large rectangle of even thickness, at least 12 inches by 9 inches. Evenly cut dough into 12 squares. Place each square in a muffin cup, and press it into the bottom and up along the sides.

Bake until golden brown, 10 to 12 minutes.

Let cool completely, about 15 minutes.

In a large bowl, fold apple mixture into Cool Whip. Evenly distribute mixture among the dough cups, and drizzle with caramel dip. Dig in!

MAKES 12 SERVINGS

96 calories per serving

✳ Flip to the photo inserts to see dozens of recipe pics! And for photos of ALL the recipes, go to **hungry-girl.com/books**.

Bananas Foster Cream Fluff Cups

You'll Need: 12-cup muffin pan, nonstick spray, large bowl, rolling pin (optional)

Prep: 20 minutes   **Cook:** 15 minutes   **Cool:** 15 minutes

1/12th of recipe (1 cream fluff cup): 111 calories, 3g fat, 227mg sodium, 20g carbs, 0.5g fiber, 7g sugars, 1g protein

Ingredients

3 tablespoons Jell-O Sugar Free Fat Free Vanilla Instant pudding mix
⅛ teaspoon cinnamon
1½ cups Cool Whip Free (thawed)
2 medium bananas
1 package refrigerated Pillsbury Crescent Recipe
    Creations Seamless Dough Sheet
3 tablespoons fat-free, low-fat, or light caramel dip

Directions

Preheat oven to 350 degrees. Spray a 12-cup muffin pan with nonstick spray.

In a large bowl, combine pudding mix with cinnamon. Add ⅓ cup cold water, and vigorously stir until mostly smooth and slightly thickened. Add Cool Whip, and stir until uniform.

Mash one banana, and stir it into the pudding mixture. Cover and refrigerate.

Roll or stretch out dough into a large rectangle of even thickness, at least 12 inches by 9 inches. Evenly cut dough into 12 squares. Place each square in a muffin cup, and press it into the bottom and up along the sides.

For a pic of this recipe, see the second photo insert. Yay!

Bake until golden brown, 10 to 12 minutes.

Let cool completely, about 15 minutes.

Gently swirl 1 tablespoon caramel dip into the pudding mixture. Evenly distribute mixture among the dough cups.

Chop remaining banana, and evenly distribute among the cups. Drizzle with remaining 2 tablespoons caramel dip, and enjoy!

MAKES 12 SERVINGS

111 calories per serving

Triple Chocolate Cream Fluff Cups

You'll Need: 12-cup muffin pan, nonstick spray, medium-large bowl, rolling pin (optional)

Prep: 15 minutes   **Cook:** 15 minutes   **Cool:** 15 minutes

1/12th of recipe (1 cream fluff cup): 105 calories, 3.5g fat, 212mg sodium, 16.5g carbs, <0.5g fiber, 4g sugars, 1.5g protein

Ingredients

2 cups Cool Whip Free (thawed)
1 packet hot cocoa mix with 20 to 25 calories
1 package refrigerated Pillsbury Crescent Recipe Creations Seamless Dough Sheet
3 sugar-free chocolate pudding snacks with 60 calories or less each
1½ tablespoons mini semi-sweet chocolate chips

Directions

Preheat oven to 350 degrees. Spray a 12-cup muffin pan with nonstick spray.

In a medium-large bowl, fold cocoa mix into Cool Whip until uniform. Cover and refrigerate.

Roll or stretch out dough into a large rectangle of even thickness, at least 12 inches by 9 inches. Evenly cut dough into 12 squares. Place each square in a muffin cup, and press it into the bottom and up along the sides.

Bake until golden brown, 10 to 12 minutes.

Let cool completely, about 15 minutes.

Evenly distribute pudding snacks among the cups, followed by the Cool Whip mixture and chocolate chips. Enjoy!

MAKES 12 SERVINGS

For a pic of this recipe, see the second photo insert. Yay!

PB&J Surprise Cups

You'll Need: 12-cup muffin pan, nonstick spray, rolling pin (optional), large bowl

Prep: 20 minutes   **Cook:** 15 minutes   **Cool:** 15 minutes

1/12th of recipe (1 PB&J cup): 133 calories, 5g fat, 177mg sodium, 18g carbs, 1g fiber, 9g sugars, 2.5g protein

Ingredients

1 package refrigerated Pillsbury Crescent Recipe Creations Seamless Dough Sheet
½ cup peanut butter baking chips, chopped
2 cups finely chopped strawberries
⅓ cup low-sugar strawberry preserves

Optional topping: Fat Free Reddi-wip

Directions

Preheat oven to 350 degrees. Spray a 12-cup muffin pan with nonstick spray.

Roll or stretch out dough into a large rectangle of even thickness, at least 12 inches by 9 inches. Evenly cut dough into 12 squares. Place each square in a muffin cup, and press it into the bottom and up along the sides.

Bake for 5 minutes. Evenly distribute chopped peanut butter chips among the dough cups.

Bake until dough is golden brown, 5 to 7 minutes.

Let cool completely, about 15 minutes.

In a large bowl, combine strawberries with preserves, and stir to coat.

Evenly distribute mixture among the dough cups. Eat up!

MAKES 12 SERVINGS

133 calories per serving

Mini Dutch Apple Pies

You'll Need: 12-cup muffin pan, nonstick spray (butter-flavored, if available), large nonstick pot, rolling pin (optional)

Prep: 30 minutes   **Cook:** 25 minutes   **Cool:** 10 minutes

1/12th of recipe (1 mini pie): 103 calories, 3g fat, 196mg sodium, 17.5g carbs, 1g fiber, 6.5g sugars, 1g protein

Ingredients

1½ tablespoons cornstarch
¼ cup Splenda No Calorie Sweetener (granulated)
1 teaspoon cinnamon
1 teaspoon lemon juice
⅛ teaspoon salt
2 cups diced Fuji apples
2 cups diced Granny Smith apples
1 tablespoon light whipped butter or light buttery spread
1 package refrigerated Pillsbury Crescent Recipe
        Creations Seamless Dough Sheet
2 sheets (8 crackers) cinnamon graham crackers, crushed

Sugar Alternative:

117 calories, 21g carbs, 10.5g sugars

Directions

Preheat oven to 350 degrees. Spray a 12-cup muffin pan with nonstick spray (butter flavored, if available).

In a large nonstick pot, combine cornstarch with ¾ cup water, and stir to dissolve. Add Splenda, cinnamon, lemon juice, salt, and apples. Stir well.

Set heat to medium. Stirring frequently, cook until apples have slightly softened and mixture is thick and gooey, 6 to 8 minutes.

Stir in butter, and remove from heat.

Roll or stretch out dough into a large rectangle of even thickness, at least 12 inches by 9 inches. Evenly cut dough into 12 squares. Place each square in a muffin cup, and press it into the bottom and up along the sides.

Evenly distribute apple mixture among the dough cups.

Bake until golden brown, 10 to 12 minutes.

Sprinkle with crushed graham crackers, and let slightly cool, about 10 minutes.

Gently remove pies from the pan, and enjoy!

MAKES 12 SERVINGS

103 calories per serving

CREAM FLUFF STACKS

Cream Fluff Stacks are a unique creation we dreamed up at the HG HQ. Once you try them, YOU'LL be the one having dreams about 'em . . .

Caramel Apple Cream Fluff Stacks

You'll Need: 2 baking sheets, nonstick spray, medium bowl, large bowl, rolling pin (optional), medium-large microwave-safe bowl

Prep: 25 minutes   **Cook:** 15 minutes   **Cool:** 10 minutes

$1/12^{th}$ of recipe (1 stack): 144 calories, 3.5g fat, 406mg sodium, 24.5g carbs, 0.5g fiber, 9.5g sugars, 3.5g protein

Ingredients

One 8-ounce tub fat-free cream cheese
One 4-serving box Jell-O Sugar Free Fat Free
    Vanilla Instant pudding mix
¼ cup Splenda No Calorie Sweetener (granulated)
½ teaspoon vanilla extract
2 cups Cool Whip Free (thawed)
1 package refrigerated Pillsbury Crescent Recipe Creations Seamless Dough Sheet
2 cups thinly sliced Fuji apples
¼ cup plus 2 tablespoons fat-free, low-fat, or light caramel dip

Sugar Alternative:

158 calories, 28.5g carbs, 13.5g sugars

Directions

Preheat oven to 350 degrees. Spray 2 baking sheets with nonstick spray.

In a medium bowl, stir cream cheese until smooth. In a large bowl, combine pudding mix with Splenda. Add vanilla extract and ½ cup cold water, and vigorously stir until mostly smooth and slightly thickened. Add Cool Whip and cream cheese, and stir until uniform. Cover and refrigerate.

Roll or stretch out dough into a large rectangle of even thickness, about 12 inches by 9 inches. Evenly cut dough into 12 squares.

Lay dough squares on the baking sheets, evenly spaced. Bake until lightly browned, 8 to 10 minutes.

Let cool completely, about 10 minutes.

Meanwhile, place apples in a medium-large microwave-safe bowl. Cover and microwave for 4 minutes, or until softened. Blot away excess moisture. Add ¼ cup caramel dip, and stir to coat.

Spread pudding mixture onto the dough squares, followed by the caramel-coated apples.

Drizzle with remaining 2 tablespoons caramel dip. Dig in!

MAKES 12 SERVINGS

144 calories per serving

Strawberry Shortcake Cream Fluff Stacks

You'll Need: 2 baking sheets, nonstick spray, 2 medium bowls, large bowl, rolling pin (optional)

Prep: 25 minutes   **Cook:** 10 minutes   **Cool:** 10 minutes

1/12ᵗʰ of recipe (1 stack): 133 calories, 3.5g fat, 377mg sodium, 21.5g carbs, 0.5g fiber, 8g sugars, 3.5g protein

Ingredients

One 8-ounce tub fat-free cream cheese
One 4-serving box Jell-O Sugar Free
    Fat Free Vanilla Instant pudding mix
¼ cup Splenda No Calorie Sweetener (granulated)
½ teaspoon vanilla extract
2 cups Cool Whip Free (thawed)
1 package refrigerated Pillsbury Crescent Recipe
    Creations Seamless Dough Sheet
2 cups sliced strawberries
½ cup low-sugar strawberry preserves

Sugar Alternative:

147 calories, 25.5g carbs, 12g sugars

Directions

Preheat oven to 350 degrees. Spray 2 baking sheets with nonstick spray.

In a medium bowl, stir cream cheese until smooth. In a large bowl, combine pudding mix with Splenda. Add vanilla extract and ½ cup cold water, and vigorously stir until mostly smooth and slightly thickened. Add Cool Whip and cream cheese, and stir until uniform. Cover and refrigerate.

Roll or stretch out dough into a large rectangle of even thickness, about 12 inches by 9 inches. Evenly cut dough into 12 squares.

Lay dough squares on the baking sheets, evenly spaced. Bake until lightly browned, 8 to 10 minutes.

Let cool completely, about 10 minutes.

Spread half of the pudding mixture onto the dough squares, and top with half of the strawberries.

Top with remaining pudding mixture and strawberries.

In a medium bowl, thoroughly mix preserves with 1 tablespoon water. Drizzle over strawberries, and enjoy!

MAKES 12 SERVINGS

133 calories per serving

For more recipes, tips & tricks, sign up for FREE daily emails at **hungry-girl.com**!

Berries & Cream Fluff Stacks

You'll Need: 2 baking sheets, nonstick spray, medium bowl, large bowl, rolling pin (optional), medium-large bowl

Prep: 25 minutes   **Cook:** 10 minutes   **Cool:** 10 minutes

1/12ᵗʰ of recipe (1 stack): 121 calories, 3.5g fat, 377mg sodium, 19g carbs, 1g fiber, 5g sugars, 3.5g protein

Ingredients

One 8-ounce tub fat-free cream cheese
One 4-serving box Jell-O Sugar Free
    Fat Free Vanilla Instant pudding mix
¼ cup Splenda No Calorie Sweetener (granulated)
½ teaspoon vanilla extract
2 cups Cool Whip Free (thawed)
1 package refrigerated Pillsbury Crescent Recipe Creations Seamless Dough Sheet
¾ cup raspberries
¾ cup blackberries
¾ cup blueberries

Optional topping: powdered sugar

Sugar Alternative:

135 calories, 22.5g carbs, 9g sugars

Directions

Preheat oven to 350 degrees. Spray 2 baking sheets with nonstick spray.

In a medium bowl, stir cream cheese until smooth. In a large bowl, combine pudding mix and Splenda. Add vanilla extract and ½ cup cold water, and vigorously stir until mostly smooth and slightly thickened. Add Cool Whip and cream cheese, and stir until uniform. Cover and refrigerate.

For a pic of this recipe, see the second photo insert. Yay!

Roll or stretch out dough into a large rectangle of even thickness, about 12 inches by 9 inches. Evenly cut dough into 12 squares.

Lay dough squares on the baking sheets, evenly spaced. Bake until lightly browned, 8 to 10 minutes.

Let cool completely, about 10 minutes.

Place berries in a medium-large bowl, and toss to mix.

Spread half of the pudding mixture onto the dough squares, and top with half of the berries.

Top with remaining pudding mixture and berries. Dig in!

MAKES 12 SERVINGS

CHAPTER 13

TRIFLES, PARFAITS & CRÈME BRÛLÉES

"Trifles, parfaits & crème brûlées . . . trifles, parfaits & crème brûlées!" Come on, chant with us! Weeeeee! These trifles are cake-y and incredible. The parfaits—layer upon layer of delicious fun. And these crème brûlées are IMPOSSIBLY amazing. (How DO we do it?!)

Rockin' Red Velvet Trifle

You'll Need: 8-inch by 8-inch baking pan, nonstick spray, glass, large bowl, whisk, cooling rack, 2 medium bowls, large glass bowl or trifle dish

Prep: 25 minutes   **Cook:** 30 minutes   **Cool:** 1 hour

1/8th of trifle (about 1 cup): 196 calories, 4g fat, 391mg sodium, 37g carbs, 2g fiber, 18g sugars, 4g protein

Ingredients

1 packet hot cocoa mix with 20 to 25 calories
2 tablespoons mini semi-sweet chocolate chips
½ cup moist-style devil's food cake mix
½ cup moist-style yellow cake mix
¼ cup fat-free liquid egg substitute
½ tablespoon red food coloring
Dash salt
4 ounces (about ½ cup) fat-free cream cheese
2 tablespoons Jell-O Sugar Free Fat Free Vanilla Instant pudding mix
2 tablespoons Splenda No Calorie Sweetener (granulated)
¼ teaspoon vanilla extract
One 8-ounce container Cool Whip Free (thawed)
4 cups chopped strawberries

Directions

Preheat oven to 350 degrees. Spray an 8-inch by 8-inch baking pan with nonstick spray.

Place cocoa mix and 1 tablespoon chocolate chips in a glass. Add ¼ cup very hot water, and stir until mostly dissolved. Add ⅓ cup cold water.

For a pic of this recipe, see the second photo insert. Yay!

In a large bowl, combine cake mixes, egg substitute, food coloring, and salt. Add cocoa mixture, and whisk until smooth.

Pour batter into the baking pan, and sprinkle with remaining 1 tablespoon chocolate chips.

Bake until a toothpick inserted into the center comes out mostly clean, 26 to 28 minutes.

Let cool completely, about 30 minutes in the pan and 30 minutes out of the pan on a cooling rack.

Meanwhile, in a medium bowl, stir cream cheese until smooth. In another medium bowl, combine pudding mix with Splenda. Add vanilla extract and ¼ cup cold water, and vigorously stir until mostly smooth and slightly thickened. Add cream cheese and 1 cup Cool Whip, and stir until uniform. Cover and refrigerate.

Cut cake into 1-inch cubes.

In a large glass bowl or trifle dish, evenly layer half of the cubed cake. Spread all of the pudding mixture over the cake layer. Evenly top with half of the strawberries.

Continue layering with remaining cubed cake, Cool Whip, and strawberries. Enjoy!

MAKES 8 SERVINGS

196 calories per serving

Berry-Good Tropical Trifle

You'll Need: 8-inch by 8-inch baking pan, nonstick spray, large bowl, whisk, cooling rack, large glass bowl or trifle dish

Prep: 20 minutes   **Cook:** 20 minutes   **Cool:** 1 hour

1/8th of trifle (about 1 cup): 188 calories, 2g fat, 202mg sodium, 41.5g carbs, 2.5g fiber, 27g sugars, 2g protein

Ingredients

1 cup moist-style yellow cake mix
¼ cup fat-free liquid egg substitute
½ teaspoon baking powder
One 20-ounce can crushed pineapple packed in juice, drained
3 cups roughly chopped strawberries
2 cups cubed mango (fresh or thawed from frozen)
1½ cups Cool Whip Free (thawed)

Directions

Preheat oven to 350 degrees. Spray an 8-inch by 8-inch baking pan with nonstick spray.

In a large bowl, combine cake mix, egg substitute, and baking powder. Add ½ cup water, and whisk until smooth. Pour batter into the pan.

Bake until a toothpick inserted into the center comes out clean, 18 to 20 minutes.

Let cool completely, about 30 minutes in the pan and 30 minutes out of the pan on a cooling rack.

Cut cake into 1-inch cubes.

In a large glass bowl or trifle dish, evenly layer half of each ingredient: cubed cake, drained pineapple, strawberries, mango, and Cool Whip.

Repeat layering with remaining ingredients. Eat up!

MAKES 8 SERVINGS

Red, White & Blueberry Trifle

You'll Need: medium-large bowl, large glass bowl or trifle dish

Prep: 15 minutes

⅛th of trifle (about 1 cup): 170 calories, 1.5g fat, 133mg sodium, 38g carbs, 3.5g fiber, 20.5g sugars, 2g protein

Ingredients

One 8-ounce container Cool Whip Free (thawed)
1 sugar-free vanilla pudding snack with 60 calories or less
Half of a 13-ounce angel food cake, cut into 1-inch cubes (about 5 cups cubed)
2 cups chopped strawberries
2 cups blueberries
2 cups raspberries

HG Alternative: If you can't find a 13-ounce angel food cake, look for a similar size. Otherwise, get any size angel food cake and use 5 cups cubed cake.

Directions

In a medium-large bowl, thoroughly fold pudding into Cool Whip.

In a large glass bowl or trifle dish, evenly layer half of each ingredient: cubed angel food cake, Cool Whip mixture, strawberries, blueberries, and raspberries.

Repeat layering with remaining ingredients. Yum!

MAKES 8 SERVINGS

170 calories per serving

Very Cherry Dreamboat Parfaits

You'll Need: 2 medium bowls, 2 mid-sized glasses
Prep: 10 minutes

¹/₂ of recipe (1 parfait): 174 calories, 2.5g fat, 517mg sodium, 31g carbs, 1.5g fiber, 15.5g sugars, 6.5g protein

Ingredients

¼ cup plus 2 tablespoons fat-free cream cheese
1½ tablespoons Jell-O Sugar Free Fat Free Vanilla Instant pudding mix
2 no-calorie sweetener packets
¼ teaspoon vanilla extract
¾ cup Cool Whip Free (thawed)
1 cup frozen unsweetened pitted dark sweet cherries, thawed and drained
4 dashes cinnamon
2 Reduced Fat Nilla Wafers, crushed

Optional topping: Fat Free Reddi-wip

Directions

In a medium bowl, stir cream cheese until smooth. In another medium bowl, combine pudding mix, sweetener, and vanilla extract. Add 3 tablespoons cold water, and vigorously stir until mostly smooth and slightly thickened. Add Cool Whip and cream cheese, and stir until uniform.

Evenly divide half of the thawed cherries between two mid-sized glasses. Evenly divide half of the pudding mixture between the glasses.

Repeat layering with remaining cherries and pudding mixture. Evenly sprinkle with cinnamon and crushed wafers. Enjoy!

MAKES 2 SERVINGS

Tropical Dreamboat Parfaits

You'll Need: 2 medium bowls, 2 mid-sized glasses
Prep: 15 minutes

¹/₂ of recipe (1 parfait): 181 calories, 2.5g fat, 516mg sodium, 32.5g carbs, 1.5g fiber, 18.5g sugars, 6.5g protein

Ingredients

¼ cup plus 2 tablespoons fat-free cream cheese
1 ½ tablespoons Jell-O Sugar Free Fat Free Vanilla Instant pudding mix
2 no-calorie sweetener packets
¼ teaspoon vanilla extract
¾ cup Cool Whip Free (thawed)
½ cup pineapple chunks packed in juice, drained
½ cup chopped mango
2 teaspoons shredded sweetened coconut

Directions

In a medium bowl, stir cream cheese until smooth. In another medium bowl, combine pudding mix, sweetener, and vanilla extract. Add 3 tablespoons cold water, and vigorously stir until mostly smooth and slightly thickened. Add Cool Whip and cream cheese, and stir until completely uniform.

Evenly divide drained pineapple between two mid-sized glasses, followed by half of the pudding mixture.

Evenly divide mango between the mid-sized glasses, followed by the remaining half of the pudding mixture.

Sprinkle with coconut and dive in!

MAKES 2 SERVINGS

📷 For a pic of this recipe, see the second photo insert. Yay!

Apple Cinnamon Dreamboat Parfaits

You'll Need: medium nonstick pot, 3 medium bowls, 2 mid-sized glasses

Prep: 25 minutes   **Cook:** 15 minutes   **Cool:** 1 hour

1/2 of recipe (1 parfait): 198 calories, 2.5g fat, 605mg sodium, 38.5g carbs, 2g fiber, 18g sugars, 6.5g protein

Ingredients

1 ¼ teaspoons cornstarch
2 cups peeled and chopped Fuji apples
Dash salt
2½ tablespoons Splenda No Calorie Sweetener (granulated)
¼ teaspoon plus ⅛ teaspoon vanilla extract
¾ teaspoon plus 1 dash cinnamon
¼ cup plus 2 tablespoons fat-free cream cheese
1½ tablespoons Jell-O Sugar Free Fat Free Vanilla Instant pudding mix
¾ cup Cool Whip Free (thawed)
2 cinnamon graham crackers (½ sheet), crushed

Optional toppings: Fat Free Reddi-wip, additional cinnamon

Directions

In a medium nonstick pot, combine cornstarch with ½ cup cold water, and stir to dissolve. Add apples, salt, 1 tablespoon Splenda, ⅛ teaspoon vanilla extract, and ¾ teaspoon cinnamon. Stir well.

Set heat to medium. Stirring frequently, cook until apples have softened and mixture is thick and gooey, 10 to 12 minutes.

Brownie-Bottomed Ice Cream Cake, p. 220

186
calories
PER SERVING

FREEZY DESSERT SANDWICHES

137 calories PER SERVING

Frozen Cannoli Sandwiches, p. 196

189 calories PER SERVING

Freezy PB Pretzel'wich Minis, p. 202

ICE CREAM CUPCAKES & OTHER FROZEN TREATS

98 calories PER SERVING

Freezy Vanilla Cupcakes, p. 214

180 calories PER SERVING

Freezy Movie Concession Stand Pie, p. 221

CRUNCHERS & CRUNCHETTES

Pumpkin Pie Crunchettes, p. 252

Blueberry Cheesecake Crunchers, p. 238

German Chocolate Crunchers, p. 244

Over the Rainbow Crunchettes, p. 251

Triple Chocolate Cream Fluff Cups, p. 286

Ooey-Gooey Apple Pie Cones, p. 265

Bananas Foster Cream Fluff Cups, p. 284

84 calories PER SERVING

105 calories PER SERVING

111 calories PER SERVING

TRIFLES, PARFAITS & CRÈME BRÛLÉES

181 calories PER SERVING

Tropical Dreamboat Parfaits, p. 303

157 calories PER SERVING

Cappuccino Crème Brûlée, p. 310

196 calories PER SERVING

Rockin' Red Velvet Trifle, p. 298

135
calories
PER SERVING

Dippy-Good Grilled Fruit Kebabs, p. 328

140
calories
PER SERVING

144
calories
PER SERVING

Baked Caramel 'n Coconut Apples, p. 324

Strawberry Shortcake Waffle Tacos, p. 336

Berries & Cream Fluff Stacks, p. 294

121 calories PER SERVING

Transfer to a medium bowl, and let cool completely, about 1 hour.

Meanwhile, in another medium bowl, stir cream cheese until smooth. In a third medium bowl, combine pudding mix with remaining 1½ tablespoons Splenda, ¼ teaspoon vanilla extract, and dash of cinnamon. Add 3 tablespoons cold water, and vigorously stir until mostly smooth and slightly thickened. Add Cool Whip and cream cheese, and stir until uniform. Cover and refrigerate.

Divide half of the apple mixture between two mid-sized glasses. Divide half of the pudding mixture between the glasses.

Repeat layering with remaining apple and pudding mixtures. Sprinkle with crushed graham crackers and enjoy!

MAKES 2 SERVINGS

198 calories per serving

Key Lime Pie-fait

You'll Need: 2 medium bowls, mid-sized glass

Prep: 10 minutes

Entire recipe: 185 calories, 3g fat, 724mg sodium, 30g carbs, 0.5g fiber, 8.5g sugars, 8.5g protein

Ingredients

¼ cup fat-free cream cheese
1 tablespoon Jell-O Sugar Free Fat Free Instant pudding mix
1 no-calorie sweetener packet
⅛ teaspoon vanilla extract
2 tablespoons key lime juice
½ cup Cool Whip Free (thawed)
2 low-fat honey graham crackers (½ sheet), lightly crushed

Directions

In a medium bowl, stir cream cheese until smooth. In another medium bowl, combine pudding mix, sweetener, and vanilla extract. Add 2 tablespoons cold water, and vigorously stir until mostly smooth and slightly thickened. Add cream cheese and lime juice, and vigorously stir until uniform.

In a mid-sized glass, layer half of each ingredient: pudding mixture, Cool Whip, and crushed graham crackers.

Repeat layering with remaining ingredients. Enjoy!

MAKES 1 SERVING

PB 'n Chocolate
Puddin' Crunch Parfait

You'll Need: mid-sized glass

Prep: 5 minutes

> **Entire recipe:** 196 calories, 5g fat, 268mg sodium, 37.5g carbs, 1g fiber, 11g sugars, 3g protein

Ingredients

1 sugar-free chocolate pudding snack with 60 calories or less
½ cup Cool Whip Free (thawed)
⅓ cup Reese's Puffs cereal
1 teaspoon mini semi-sweet chocolate chips

Directions

In a mid-sized glass, layer half of the following ingredients: pudding, Cool Whip, and cereal.

Repeat layering with remaining pudding, Cool Whip, and cereal. Sprinkle with chocolate chips, grab a spoon, and dig in!

MAKES 1 SERVING

Crunchy Caramel Apple Layer Parfaits

You'll Need: medium bowl, whisk, large bowl, 4 mid-sized glasses

Prep: 15 minutes

1/4th of recipe (1 parfait): 199 calories, 1.5g fat, 324mg sodium, 44g carbs, 2g fiber, 23g sugars, 4g protein

Ingredients

¼ cup fat-free cream cheese
1 tablespoon granulated white sugar
2 tablespoons fat-free ricotta cheese
2 tablespoons fat-free, low-fat, or light caramel dip
Drop vanilla extract
2 cups diced Fuji apples
1 teaspoon cinnamon
1 teaspoon brown sugar
1½ cups Cool Whip Free (thawed)
28 mini caramel rice cakes, lightly crushed

No-Calorie Sweetener Alternative:

190 calories, 41g carbs, 20g sugars

Directions

In a medium bowl, stir cream cheese with sugar until smooth. Add ricotta cheese, caramel dip, and vanilla extract. Vigorously whisk until uniform.

In a large bowl, sprinkle apples with cinnamon and brown sugar, and stir to coat.

Evenly distribute half of the apple mixture among 4 mid-sized glasses, followed by half of the Cool Whip and half of the rice cakes.

Evenly distribute all of the cream cheese mixture among the glasses.

Continue layering with remaining apple mixture, Cool Whip, and rice cakes. Yay!

MAKES 4 SERVINGS

CRÈME BRÛLÉE TIPS 'N TRICKS . . .

Find 6-ounce ramekins at Bed Bath & Beyond, kitchen supply stores, and online.

When removing your ramekins from the water bath, large sturdy tongs are a great tool to help you avoid burning your hands. And after torching the top of your crème brûlée, have an oven mitt or towel handy, since the ramekin may be hot.

Sugar is essential for crème brûlée. (Sugar substitutes don't work in these recipes.) Sprinkle the sweet stuff evenly across the tops of your custard cups before torching to ensure that every bite gets a bit of crisp caramelized sugar.

Cappuccino Crème Brûlée

You'll Need: four 6-ounce baking ramekins (or custard cups) 3½ inches in diameter, 9-inch by 13-inch baking pan, medium pot, large bowl, whisk, handheld butane kitchen torch

Prep: 15 minutes   **Cook:** 55 minutes   **Cool/Chill:** 3 hours

¼th of recipe (1 ramekin): 157 calories, 1g fat, 182mg sodium, 27.5g carbs, 0g fiber, 25g sugars, 7g protein

Ingredients

¾ cup fat-free evaporated milk
¾ cup fat-free half & half
¼ cup plus 1 tablespoon brown sugar (not packed)
2¼ teaspoons sugar-free French vanilla powdered creamer
¾ teaspoon instant coffee granules
½ cup fat-free liquid egg substitute
1¾ teaspoons vanilla extract
4 teaspoons granulated white sugar
½ cup Fat Free Reddi-wip

Directions

Preheat oven to 300 degrees. Set four 6-ounce baking ramekins (or custard cups), each about 3½ inches in diameter, in a 9-inch by 13-inch baking pan.

In a medium pot, mix evaporated milk, half & half, brown sugar, powdered creamer, and coffee granules. Set temperature to medium. Cook and stir until sugar and powdered creamer have dissolved and mixture is hot and begins to steam, about 5 minutes. Remove from heat.

In a large bowl, mix egg substitute with vanilla extract. Gradually whisk in the hot milk mixture.

For a pic of this recipe, see the second photo insert. Yay!

Evenly distribute mixture among the ramekins.

Pour hot water into the baking pan, around the ramekins, until it reaches about halfway up the outsides of the ramekins.

Carefully transfer pan to the oven, and bake until custards are just set, about 45 minutes.

Carefully remove ramekins from the baking pan, and let cool completely, about 1 hour.

Refrigerate until chilled, at least 2 hours.

Once ready to serve, if needed, blot away excess moisture. Top each ramekin with 1 teaspoon white sugar. Using a handheld butane kitchen torch, caramelize the sugar (blast it with fire 'til browned).

Let caramelized sugar harden. Just before serving, top each ramekin with a 2-tablespoon squirt of Reddi-wip, and enjoy!

MAKES 4 SERVINGS

157 calories per serving

Coconut Crème Brûlée

You'll Need: four 6-ounce baking ramekins (or custard cups) 3½ inches in diameter, 9-inch by 13-inch baking pan, medium pot, large bowl, whisk, handheld butane kitchen torch

Prep: 15 minutes   **Cook:** 55 minutes   **Cool/Chill:** 3 hours

1/4th of recipe (1 ramekin): 187 calories, 3g fat, 204mg sodium, 30g carbs, 1g fiber, 27g sugars, 7.5g protein

Ingredients

¾ cup fat-free evaporated milk
¾ cup fat-free half & half
¼ cup plus 1 tablespoon brown sugar (not packed)
2¼ teaspoons sugar-free French vanilla powdered creamer
½ cup fat-free liquid egg substitute
1½ teaspoons vanilla extract
¼ teaspoon coconut extract
4 teaspoons granulated white sugar
¼ cup shredded sweetened coconut

Directions

Preheat oven to 300 degrees. Set four 6-ounce baking ramekins (or custard cups), each about 3½ inches in diameter, in a 9-inch by 13-inch baking pan.

In a medium pot, mix evaporated milk, half & half, brown sugar, and powdered creamer. Set temperature to medium. Cook and stir until sugar and powdered creamer have dissolved and mixture is hot and begins to steam, about 5 minutes. Remove from heat.

In a large bowl, mix egg substitute, vanilla extract, and coconut extract. Gradually whisk the hot milk mixture into the egg mixture.

Evenly distribute mixture among the ramekins.

Pour hot water into the baking pan, around the ramekins, until it reaches about halfway up the outsides of the ramekins.

Carefully transfer pan to the oven, and bake until custards are just set, about 45 minutes.

Carefully remove ramekins from the baking pan, and let cool completely, about 1 hour.

Refrigerate until chilled, at least 2 hours.

Once ready to serve, if needed, blot away excess moisture. Top each ramekin with 1 teaspoon white sugar. Using a handheld butane kitchen torch, caramelize the sugar (blast it with fire 'til browned).

Sprinkle with shredded coconut. Eat up!

MAKES 4 SERVINGS

187 calories per serving

* Flip to the photo inserts to see dozens of recipe pics! And for photos of ALL the recipes, go to **hungry-girl.com/books.**

Sugar and Spice Crème Brûlée

You'll Need: four 6-ounce baking ramekins (or custard cups) 3½ inches in diameter, 9-inch by 13-inch baking pan, medium pot, large bowl, whisk, handheld butane kitchen torch

Prep: 15 minutes   **Cook:** 55 minutes   **Cool/Chill:** 3 hours

1/4th of recipe (1 ramekin): 152 calories, 1g fat, 182mg sodium, 26.5g carbs, <0.5g fiber, 24.5g sugars, 7g protein

Ingredients

¾ cup fat-free evaporated milk
¾ cup fat-free half & half
¼ cup plus 1 tablespoon brown sugar (not packed)
2¼ teaspoons sugar-free French vanilla powdered creamer
½ cup fat-free liquid egg substitute
1½ teaspoons vanilla extract
¼ teaspoon maple extract
⅛ teaspoon cinnamon
⅛ teaspoon pumpkin pie spice
4 teaspoons granulated white sugar

Directions

Preheat oven to 300 degrees. Set four 6-ounce baking ramekins (or custard cups), each about 3½ inches in diameter, in a 9-inch by 13-inch baking pan.

In a medium pot, mix evaporated milk, half & half, brown sugar, and powdered creamer. Set temperature to medium. Cook and stir until sugar and powdered creamer have dissolved and mixture is hot and begins to steam, about 5 minutes. Remove from heat.

In a large bowl, mix egg substitute, vanilla extract, and maple extract. Gradually whisk the hot milk mixture into the egg mixture.

Evenly distribute mixture among the ramekins. Pour hot water into the baking pan, around the ramekins, until it reaches about halfway up the outsides of the ramekins.

Carefully transfer pan to the oven, and bake until custards are just set, about 45 minutes.

Carefully remove ramekins from the baking pan, and let cool completely, about 1 hour.

Refrigerate until chilled, at least 2 hours.

Once ready to serve, if needed, blot away excess moisture. Sprinkle with cinnamon and pumpkin pie spice, followed by white sugar. Using a handheld butane kitchen torch, caramelize the sugar (blast it with fire 'til browned). Dive in!

MAKES 4 SERVINGS

152 calories per serving

CHAPTER 14

FRUITY FUN

Baked fruit, grilled fruit, gooey fruit . . . All here for your
chewing pleasure!

Stuffed-Apple Apple Pie

You'll Need: 8-inch by 8-inch baking pan, nonstick spray, melon baller (optional), medium bowl, aluminum foil, small bowl

Prep: 10 minutes   **Cook:** 35 minutes

Entire recipe: 182 calories, 2g fat, 203mg sodium, 43g carbs, 6g fiber, 31g sugars, 1g protein

Ingredients

1 large Granny Smith apple
½ no-calorie sweetener packet
¼ teaspoon cinnamon
Dash salt
2¼ teaspoons brown sugar (not packed)
1 cinnamon graham cracker (¼ sheet), lightly crushed
½ tablespoon old-fashioned oats
¾ teaspoon light whipped butter or light buttery spread, room temperature

Directions

Preheat oven to 375 degrees. Spray an 8-inch by 8-inch baking pan with nonstick spray.

Slice off the top of the apple, about ½ inch. Carefully hollow out most of the inside flesh with a spoon or melon baller, leaving about ¼ inch of flesh on the skin, and leaving the bottom intact. Discard seeds and core.

Chop the scooped-out flesh, and place it in a medium bowl. Sprinkle with sweetener, cinnamon, and salt. Add 1½ teaspoons brown sugar, and stir to coat. Place mixture in the hollow apple, and lightly pack with the back of a spoon.

Place apple in the baking pan. Cover pan with foil, and bake for 30 minutes.

In a small bowl, combine crushed graham cracker, oats, butter, and remaining ¾ teaspoon brown sugar. Mash and stir until well mixed and crumbly.

Remove foil. Sprinkle graham mixture over the apple.

Bake, uncovered, until graham mixture has lightly browned, about 5 minutes. Eat!

MAKES 1 SERVING

182 calories per serving

For more recipes, tips & tricks, sign up for FREE daily emails at **hungry-girl.com!**

Caramel-Drizzled Caramelized Pineapple

You'll Need: grill pan, nonstick spray, plate

Prep: 5 minutes   **Cook:** 10 minutes

¹/₂ of recipe (4 rings): 149 calories, <0.5g fat, 44mg sodium, 38g carbs, 2.5g fiber, 30g sugars, 0.5g protein

Ingredients

8 pineapple rings, fresh or packed in juice and drained
½ teaspoon cinnamon
1 tablespoon fat-free, low-fat, or light caramel dip

Directions

Bring a grill pan sprayed with nonstick spray to medium heat.

Sprinkle pineapple rings on both sides with cinnamon, and cook until slightly blackened and caramelized, about 4 minutes per side, flipping carefully.

Plate rings, drizzle with caramel dip, and devour!

MAKES 2 SERVINGS

Cherry-Picked
Fake-Baked Apple

You'll Need: apple corer, deep medium-sized microwave-safe bowl

Prep: 5 minutes   **Cook:** 5 minutes

Entire recipe: 115 calories, <0.5g fat, 27mg sodium, 31g carbs, 4.5g fiber, 22.5g sugars, 0.5g protein

Ingredients

1 medium Rome apple
2 maraschino cherries
½ cup diet cherry-vanilla cream soda
½ no-calorie sweetener packet
Dash cinnamon

Directions

Core apple. Place in a deep medium-sized microwave-safe bowl. Place cherries in the cored center of the apple. Pour soda over the apple, and sprinkle with sweetener and cinnamon.

Cover and microwave for 4 minutes, or until tender.

Enjoy hot, warm, or cold!

MAKES 1 SERVING

Craisin'-Amazin' Baked Apples

You'll Need: apple corer, 8-inch by 8-inch baking pan

Prep: 5 minutes   **Cook:** 55 minutes

1/4th of recipe (1 apple): 108 calories, <0.5g fat, 19mg sodium, 28.5g carbs, 4.5g fiber, 21g sugars, 0.5g protein

Ingredients

4 medium Rome apples
2 tablespoons dried sweetened cranberries
One 12-ounce can diet cream soda
2 no-calorie sweetener packets
¼ teaspoon cinnamon

Optional toppings: Fat-Free Reddi-wip, additional cinnamon

Directions

Preheat oven to 375 degrees.

Core apples and place in an 8-inch by 8-inch baking pan. Evenly distribute cranberries among the cored centers of the apples. Pour soda over the apples. Sprinkle with sweetener and cinnamon.

Bake until apples are tender, 45 to 55 minutes. Enjoy!

MAKES 4 SERVINGS

Raisin' the Roof Baked Apples

You'll Need: apple corer, 8-inch by 8-inch baking pan

Prep: 5 minutes   **Cook:** 55 minutes

1/4ᵗʰ of recipe (1 apple): 112 calories, <0.5g fat, 13mg sodium, 29g carbs, 4.5g fiber, 22g sugars, 0.5g protein

Ingredients

4 medium Rome apples
2 tablespoons raisins
One 12-ounce can diet black cherry soda
2 no-calorie sweetener packets
¼ teaspoon cinnamon

Optional toppings: Fat-Free Reddi-wip, additional cinnamon

Directions

Preheat oven to 375 degrees.

Core apples and place in an 8-inch by 8-inch baking pan. Evenly distribute raisins among the cored centers of the apples. Pour soda over the apples. Sprinkle with sweetener and cinnamon.

Bake until apples are tender, 45 to 55 minutes. Eat up!

MAKES 4 SERVINGS

Baked Caramel 'n Coconut Apples

You'll Need: apple corer, 8-inch by 8-inch baking pan

Prep: 10 minutes   **Cook:** 55 minutes

> **¼th of recipe (1 apple):** 140 calories, 1.5g fat, 53mg sodium, 34g carbs, 5g fiber, 24g sugars, 0.5g protein

Ingredients

4 medium Rome apples
One 12-ounce can diet black cherry soda
2 no-calorie sweetener packets
¼ teaspoon cinnamon
2 tablespoons fat-free, low-fat, or light caramel dip
2 tablespoons shredded sweetened coconut

Directions

Preheat oven to 375 degrees.

Core apples and place in an 8-inch by 8-inch baking pan. Pour soda over the apples. Sprinkle with sweetener and cinnamon.

Bake until apples are tender, 45 to 55 minutes.

Once cool enough to handle, remove apples, and vertically cut into halves. Drizzle with caramel dip and sprinkle with shredded coconut. Enjoy!

MAKES 4 SERVINGS

For a pic of this recipe, see the second photo insert. Yay!

Streuseled-Up
Baked Peaches

You'll Need: 8-inch by 8-inch baking pan, nonstick spray, medium bowl

Prep: 10 minutes   **Cook:** 15 minutes

> **¹/₂ of recipe (2 peach halves):** 192 calories, 5.5g fat, 55mg sodium, 33g carbs, 3g fiber, 19g sugars, 3g protein

192 calories per serving

Ingredients

4 peach halves packed in juice, drained and blotted dry
3 tablespoons old-fashioned oats
2 tablespoons whole-wheat flour
2 tablespoons brown sugar (not packed)
1 tablespoon light whipped butter or light buttery spread
1 tablespoon chopped pecans
¾ teaspoon cinnamon

Directions

Preheat oven to 400 degrees. Spray an 8-inch by 8-inch baking pan with nonstick spray.

Place peach halves in the pan, cut sides up.

In a medium bowl, combine remaining ingredients. Mash and stir until well mixed and crumbly. Evenly distribute among the peach halves.

Bake until topping is firm, 10 to 12 minutes. Eat up!

MAKES 2 SERVINGS

Crazy-Amazing Pineapple Grillers with Coconut Dip

You'll Need: medium bowl, grill pan, nonstick spray

Prep: 5 minutes **Cook:** 20 minutes

> **¼th of recipe (4 pineapple rings with about 3 tablespoons dip):**
> 192 calories, 2g fat, 54mg sodium, 39g carbs, 3.5g fiber, 33g sugars,
> 5g protein

Ingredients

Dip
6 ounces (about ⅔ cup) fat-free plain Greek yogurt
¼ cup shredded sweetened coconut
1 tablespoon granulated white sugar
⅛ teaspoon coconut extract

No-Calorie Sweetener Alternative:

182 calories, 36.5g carbs, 30g sugars

Pineapple
16 pineapple rings, fresh or packed in juice and drained

Directions

In a medium bowl, mix dip ingredients until uniform. Cover and refrigerate.

Bring a grill pan sprayed with nonstick spray to medium heat. Working in batches, cook pineapple rings until slightly blackened and caramelized, about 4 minutes per side, flipping carefully.

Serve pineapple rings with dip, and devour!

MAKES 4 SERVINGS

192 calories per serving

Sugar 'n Spice Baked Pears

You'll Need: apple corer, 9-inch by 13-inch baking pan

Prep: 5 minutes   **Cook:** 35 minutes

¼th of recipe (1 pear): 110 calories, <0.5g fat, 20mg sodium, 29g carbs, 5.5g fiber, 19g sugars, 0.5g protein

Ingredients

4 medium pears (Bosc pears work great!)
Two 12-ounce cans diet black cherry soda
2 teaspoons brown sugar (not packed)
¼ teaspoon cinnamon

Optional toppings: Fat-Free Reddi-wip, additional cinnamon

Directions

Preheat oven to 375 degrees.

Core pears and halve lengthwise. Place pear halves in a 9-inch by 13-inch baking pan, cut sides up. Pour soda over pear halves, and sprinkle with brown sugar and cinnamon.

Bake until tender, about 35 minutes. Enjoy!

MAKES 4 SERVINGS

110 calories per serving

Dippy-Good Grilled Fruit Kebabs

You'll Need: 4 skewers, medium bowl, grill pan with lid, nonstick spray

Prep: 30 minutes   **Cook:** 10 minutes

1/4ᵗʰ of recipe (1 kebab with about 3 tablespoons dip): 135 calories, 0.5g fat, 17mg sodium, 30.5g carbs, 3g fiber, 23g sugars, 4.5g protein

Ingredients

Dip
6 ounces (about ⅔ cup) fat-free
    plain Greek yogurt
1 tablespoon granulated white sugar
⅛ teaspoon cinnamon
⅛ teaspoon vanilla extract

Kebabs
1 cup 1-inch pineapple chunks
1 cup 1-inch mango chunks
1 cup 1-inch peach or nectarine chunks
1 cup 1-inch banana chunks
¼ teaspoon cinnamon

No-Calorie Sweetener Alternative:

124 calories, 28g carbs, 20g sugars

Directions

If using wooden skewers, soak them in water for about 20 minutes to prevent burning.

In a medium bowl, mix dip ingredients until uniform. Cover and refrigerate.

📷 For a pic of this recipe, see the second photo insert. Yay!

Alternately skewer fruit chunks onto the skewers. Sprinkle with cinnamon.

Bring a grill pan sprayed with nonstick spray to medium heat. Add skewers, cover, and cook until fruit chunks are slightly blackened and caramelized, 3 to 5 minutes per side.

Serve grilled fruit with dip, and enjoy!

MAKES 4 SERVINGS

HG FYI:
Don't worry if the lid used for covering the pan isn't a perfect fit!

135 calories per serving

Pumpkin-Pie Apple Shakers

You'll Need: apple corer, sealable plastic bag or container

Prep: 5 minutes

Entire recipe: 100 calories, 0.5g fat, 2mg sodium, 26g carbs, 4.5g fiber, 18.5g sugars, 0.5g protein

Ingredients

1 medium Fuji apple
½ teaspoon pumpkin pie spice
1 no-calorie sweetener packet

Directions

Core apple, and cut into bite-sized chunks. Place in a sealable plastic bag or container.

Sprinkle with pumpkin pie spice and sweetener. Seal and shake until evenly distributed. Eat up!

MAKES 1 SERVING

100 calories per serving

Sweet Cinnamon Pear Shakers

You'll Need: apple corer, sealable plastic bag or container

Prep: 5 minutes

Entire recipe: 109 calories, <0.5g fat, 2mg sodium, 29g carbs, 5.5g fiber, 17.5g sugars, 0.5g protein

Ingredients

1 medium pear
¼ teaspoon cinnamon
1 no-calorie sweetener packet

Directions

Core pear, and cut into bite-sized chunks. Place in a sealable plastic bag or container.

Sprinkle with cinnamon and sweetener. Seal and shake until evenly distributed. Mmmm!!!

MAKES 1 SERVING

109
calories per serving

Stuffed-with-Love Strawberries

You'll Need: 2 medium bowls, plastic bag, scissors

Prep: 10 minutes

> **Entire recipe:** 173 calories, 4g fat, 309mg sodium, 30g carbs, 3.5g fiber, 16.5g sugars, 5.5g protein

Ingredients

2 tablespoons fat-free cream cheese
½ tablespoon Jell-O Sugar Free Fat Free Vanilla Instant pudding mix
1 no-calorie sweetener packet
1 drop vanilla extract
¼ cup Cool Whip Free (thawed)
6 extra-large strawberries
2 teaspoons mini semi-sweet chocolate chips

Directions

In a medium bowl, stir cream cheese until smooth.

In another medium bowl, combine pudding mix with sweetener. Add vanilla extract and 1 tablespoon cold water, and vigorously stir until mostly smooth and slightly thickened. Stir in Cool Whip and cream cheese until uniform.

Slice the stem ends off the strawberries, about ½ inch. Use a narrow spoon to remove about half of the flesh inside each berry, allowing room for filling.

Spoon pudding mixture into a bottom corner of a plastic bag. Snip off the tip of that corner to create a small hole, and pipe the mixture through the hole into the strawberries.

Press chocolate chips into the exposed filling. Enjoy!

MAKES 1 SERVING

Creamy Dreamy Fruit Fandango

You'll Need: apple corer, large bowl

Prep: 15 minutes

> **⅛th of recipe (about 1 cup):** 131 calories, 3g fat, 67mg sodium, 26g carbs, 3g fiber, 18.5g sugars, 1.5g protein

Ingredients

2 Granny Smith apples
3 cups seedless red grapes
1 tablespoon Jell-O Sugar Free Fat Free Vanilla Instant pudding mix
1 cup Cool Whip Free (thawed)
2 cups chopped strawberries
¼ cup thinly sliced dry-roasted almonds
2 tablespoons mini semi-sweet chocolate chips

Directions

Core and chop apples. Cut grapes into halves.

Place pudding mix in a large bowl. Add 2 tablespoons cold water, and vigorously stir until mostly smooth and slightly thickened. Add Cool Whip, and stir until uniform.

Add all of the fruit, and toss to coat. Gently stir in almonds and chocolate chips. Eat up!

MAKES 8 SERVINGS

Hungry for More?
Flip to page 364 for ALL the fruit-tastic desserts!

131 calories per serving

CHAPTER 15

DESSERTS IN DISGUISE

Psssst . . . These desserts are pretending to be some other type of delicious food, but they're really super-tasty desserts. Pizza? Nachos? How wonderfully weird!

Strawberry Shortcake Waffle Tacos

You'll Need: medium bowl, rolling pin, 9-inch by 5-inch loaf pan

Prep: 10 minutes   **Cook:** 10 minutes   **Cool:** 10 minutes

> **½ of recipe (1 waffle taco):** 144 calories, 2g fat, 196mg sodium, 29.5g carbs, 3g fiber, 9g sugars, 3g protein

Ingredients

1 tablespoon low-sugar strawberry preserves
1 no-calorie sweetener packet
¾ cup chopped strawberries
2 frozen low-fat waffles, thawed
½ cup Cool Whip Free (thawed)

Directions

Preheat oven to 425 degrees.

In a medium bowl, thoroughly mix preserves with sweetener. Add strawberries, and stir to coat. Cover and refrigerate.

Lay waffles flat on a dry surface. With a rolling pin, flatten waffles as much as possible. Evenly drape a waffle over each side of a 9-inch by 5-inch loaf pan, so they resemble upside-down tacos.

Bake until crispy and firm, about 10 minutes.

Remove from pan, and let cool completely, about 10 minutes.

Evenly divide strawberry mixture between waffle taco shells, and top with Cool Whip. Chomp!

MAKES 2 SERVINGS

For a pic of this recipe, see the second photo insert. Yay!

Banana Split Waffle Tacos

You'll Need: medium bowl, rolling pin, 9-inch by 5-inch loaf pan

Prep: 10 minutes   **Cook:** 10 minutes   **Cool:** 10 minutes

> **1/2 of recipe (1 waffle taco):** 198 calories, 4g fat, 277mg sodium, 39.5g carbs, 3.5g fiber, 11g sugars, 3.5g protein

Ingredients

1 sugar-free vanilla pudding snack with 60 calories or less
⅓ cup Cool Whip Free (thawed)
1 small banana, sliced into coins
2 frozen low-fat waffles, thawed
1 teaspoon chopped peanuts
1 teaspoon mini semi-sweet chocolate chips
2 tablespoons chopped strawberries

Directions

Preheat oven to 425 degrees.

Place pudding in a medium bowl. Fold in ¼ cup Cool Whip until uniform. Fold in banana coins. Cover and refrigerate.

Lay waffles flat on a dry surface. With a rolling pin, flatten waffles as much as possible. Evenly drape a waffle over each side of a 9-inch by 5-inch loaf pan, so they resemble upside-down tacos.

Bake until crispy and firm, about 10 minutes.

Remove from pan, and let cool completely, about 10 minutes.

Evenly divide pudding mixture between waffle taco shells, followed by remaining Cool Whip (2 teaspoons each). Top with peanuts, chocolate chips, and strawberries. Enjoy!

MAKES 2 SERVINGS

Tropical Fruit Waffle Tacos

You'll Need: rolling pin, 9-inch by 5-inch loaf pan, medium bowl

Prep: 10 minutes   **Cook:** 10 minutes   **Cool:** 10 minutes

¹/₂ of recipe (1 waffle taco): 157 calories, 2.5g fat, 204mg sodium, 31.5g carbs, 3.5g fiber, 12.5g sugars, 3g protein

Ingredients

2 frozen low-fat waffles, thawed
¼ cup canned pineapple chunks packed in juice, drained and chopped
¼ cup chopped banana
¼ cup chopped mango
¼ cup Cool Whip Free (thawed)
1 tablespoon shredded sweetened coconut

Directions

Preheat oven to 425 degrees.

Lay waffles flat on a dry surface. With a rolling pin, flatten waffles as much as possible. Evenly drape a waffle over each side of a 9-inch by 5-inch loaf pan, so they resemble upside-down tacos.

Bake until crispy and firm, about 10 minutes.

Remove from pan, and let cool completely, about 10 minutes.

Place all fruit in a medium bowl, and toss to mix.

Evenly divide fruit mixture between waffle taco shells. Top with Cool Whip and shredded coconut. Yum!

MAKES 2 SERVINGS

DIY Choco-Mallow Coconut Nachos

You'll Need: baking sheet, nonstick spray, medium bowl

Prep: 10 minutes   **Cook:** 5 minutes   **Cool:** 5 minutes

> **Entire recipe:** 168 calories, 4g fat, 317mg sodium, 33g carbs, 2g fiber, 5.5g sugars, 4g protein

Ingredients

1 sugar-free chocolate pudding snack with 60 calories or less
1 drop coconut extract
8 mini marshmallows, chopped
1 tablespoon shredded sweetened coconut
1 large square egg roll wrapper

Directions

Preheat oven to 375 degrees. Spray a baking sheet with nonstick spray.

In a medium bowl, mix coconut extract into pudding. Stir in chopped marshmallows and shredded coconut. Cover and refrigerate.

Evenly cut egg roll wrapper into 8 wedges. Lay wedges flat on the baking sheet, and bake for 2 minutes.

Carefully flip wedges and bake until lightly browned, about 2 more minutes.

Let cool completely, about 5 minutes.

Serve with pudding mixture for dipping!

MAKES 1 SERVING

168 calories per serving

DIY Banana & PB Nachos

You'll Need: baking sheet, nonstick spray, medium bowl

Prep: 10 minutes   **Cook:** 5 minutes   **Cool:** 5 minutes

> **Entire recipe:** 184 calories, 4.5g fat, 159mg sodium, 32g carbs, 1.5g fiber, 10.5g sugars, 4g protein

Ingredients

⅓ cup Cool Whip Free (thawed)
2 tablespoons finely chopped banana
2½ teaspoons peanut butter baking chips, crushed
1 large square egg roll wrapper

Directions

Preheat oven to 375 degrees. Spray a baking sheet with nonstick spray.

Place Cool Whip in a medium bowl. Fold in banana and crushed peanut butter chips. Cover and refrigerate.

Evenly cut egg roll wrapper into 8 wedges. Lay wedges flat on the baking sheet, and bake for 2 minutes.

Carefully flip wedges and bake until lightly browned, about 2 more minutes.

Let cool completely, about 5 minutes.

Serve with Cool Whip mixture for dipping!

MAKES 1 SERVING

DIY Cannoli Nachos

You'll Need: baking sheet, nonstick spray, medium bowl, whisk

Prep: 10 minutes   **Cook:** 5 minutes   **Cool:** 5 minutes

Entire recipe: 168 calories, 3g fat, 265mg sodium, 28g carbs, 1g fiber, 10.5g sugars, 7g protein

Ingredients

1 teaspoon Jell-O Sugar Free Fat Free Vanilla Instant pudding mix
3 tablespoons fat-free ricotta cheese
1½ tablespoons Cool Whip Free (thawed)
1 teaspoon powdered sugar
1 drop vanilla extract
2 teaspoons mini semi-sweet chocolate chips
1 large square egg roll wrapper

Directions

Preheat oven to 375 degrees. Spray a baking sheet with nonstick spray.

Place pudding mix in a medium bowl. Add 1 tablespoon water, and vigorously stir until mostly smooth and slightly thickened. Add ricotta cheese, Cool Whip, sugar, and vanilla extract. Stir until smooth. Stir in chocolate chips. Cover and refrigerate.

Evenly cut egg roll wrapper into 8 wedges. Lay wedges flat on the baking sheet, and bake for 2 minutes.

Carefully flip wedges and bake until lightly browned, about 2 more minutes.

Let cool completely, about 5 minutes.

Serve with pudding mixture for dipping!

MAKES 1 SERVING

168 calories per serving

DIY Apple Pie Nachos

You'll Need: baking sheet, nonstick spray, medium microwave-safe bowl
Prep: 10 minutes   **Cook:** 10 minutes   **Cool:** 5 minutes

Entire recipe: 167 calories, 1g fat, 279mg sodium, 39g carbs, 3g fiber, 17.5g sugars, 2g protein

Ingredients

1 large square egg roll wrapper
¼ teaspoon plus ⅛ teaspoon cinnamon
1 teaspoon cornstarch
¾ cup finely chopped Fuji apple
2 teaspoons brown sugar (not packed)
Dash salt
3 tablespoons Cool Whip Free (thawed)

Directions

Preheat oven to 375 degrees. Spray a baking sheet with nonstick spray.

Evenly cut egg roll wrapper into 8 wedges. Lay wedges flat on the baking sheet, and sprinkle with ⅛ teaspoon cinnamon. Bake for 2 minutes.

Carefully flip wedges, and sprinkle with another ⅛ teaspoon cinnamon. Bake until lightly browned, about 2 more minutes.

Let cool completely, about 5 minutes.

In a medium microwave-safe bowl, combine cornstarch with 3 tablespoons cold water, and stir to dissolve. Add apples, brown sugar, remaining ⅛ teaspoon cinnamon, and salt. Stir to coat.

Cover and microwave for 2 minutes.

Stir well. Cover and microwave for 2 more minutes, or until apples have softened and mixture is hot and gooey.

Serve crispy wedges with Cool Whip and warm apple mixture for dipping!

MAKES 1 SERVING

167

calories per serving

Crazy for Caramel Apple Pizza

You'll Need: baking sheet, nonstick spray, small bowl, microwave-safe bowl

Prep: 10 minutes   **Cook:** 15 minutes

> **Entire recipe:** 183 calories, 3g fat, 506mg sodium, 38.5g carbs, 7g fiber, 10.5g sugars, 8.5g protein

Ingredients

1 medium-large high-fiber flour tortilla with 110 calories or less
1½ tablespoons fat-free cream cheese
⅛ teaspoon cinnamon
¼ cup thinly sliced and roughly chopped Fuji apple
2 teaspoons fat-free, low-fat, or light caramel dip

Directions

Preheat oven to 375 degrees. Spray a baking sheet with nonstick spray.

Lay tortilla on the sheet and bake until slightly crisp, about 5 minutes.

Flip tortilla and bake until crisp, about 5 more minutes.

Meanwhile, in a small bowl, mix cream cheese with cinnamon until uniform.

In a covered microwave-safe bowl, microwave apple for 1½ minutes, or until softened. Blot away excess moisture.

Add caramel to softened apple, and stir to coat.

Spread tortilla with cream cheese mixture, leaving a ½-inch border. Top with apple mixture, and enjoy!

MAKES 1 SERVING

Sassy S'mores Quesadilla

You'll Need: skillet, nonstick spray

Prep: 5 minutes   **Cook:** 5 minutes

Entire recipe: 159 calories, 3.5g fat, 256mg sodium, 29.5g carbs, 9g fiber, 11.5g sugars, 3.5g protein

Ingredients

One 6-inch high-fiber flour tortilla with 80 calories or less
2 tablespoons Jet-Puffed Marshmallow Creme
1 teaspoon mini semi-sweet chocolate chips
1 low-fat honey graham cracker (¼ sheet), crushed

Directions

Lay tortilla flat, and spread with marshmallow creme.

Sprinkle one half of the tortilla with chocolate chips and crushed graham cracker. Fold the creme-only half over the chocolate-graham-topped half, and press lightly to seal.

Bring a skillet sprayed with nonstick spray to medium-high heat. Cook quesadilla until slightly crispy on the outside and hot on the inside, about 2 minutes per side. Mmmm!

MAKES 1 SERVING

159 calories per serving

Pumpkin Pie Pot Stickers

You'll Need: medium bowl, large skillet, nonstick spray

Prep: 20 minutes   **Cook:** 15 minutes

¼th of recipe (4 pot stickers): 137 calories, 3g fat, 220mg sodium, 23.5g carbs, 2g fiber, 3.5g sugars, 3g protein

Ingredients

½ cup canned pure pumpkin

1 sugar-free vanilla pudding snack with 60 calories or less

1 teaspoon granulated white sugar

½ teaspoon pumpkin pie spice

½ teaspoon cinnamon

Dash salt

2 tablespoons finely chopped walnuts

16 small square wonton wrappers

½ cup Fat Free Reddi-wip

Optional topping: additional cinnamon

No-Calorie Sweetener Alternative:

133 calories, 22.5g carbs, 2.5g sugars

Directions

To make the filling, in a medium bowl, combine pumpkin, pudding, sugar, pumpkin pie spice, cinnamon, and salt. Stir until uniform. Mix in walnuts.

Lay a wonton wrapper flat on a dry surface. Place a little less than a tablespoon of filling (1/16th of the filling) in the center. Moisten all four edges by dabbing your fingers in water and going over the edges smoothly. Fold the bottom left corner to meet the top right corner, forming a triangle and enclosing the filling. Press firmly on the edges to seal.

Repeat with remaining wrappers and filling.

Bring a large skillet sprayed with nonstick spray to medium-high heat. Working in batches, place pot stickers flat in the skillet, evenly spaced, and cook until lightly browned, 2 to 3 minutes per side. (Between batches, remove skillet from heat and re-spray.)

Just before serving, top each serving with 2 tablespoons Reddi-wip. Dig in!

MAKES 4 SERVINGS

137 calories per serving

Dreamy PB Chocolate Ravioli Puffs

You'll Need: medium bowl, large skillet, nonstick spray

Prep: 20 minutes   **Cook:** 10 minutes

1/4th of recipe (4 ravioli puffs): 157 calories, 4g fat, 270mg sodium, 26g carbs, 1g fiber, 1.5g sugars, 5g protein

Ingredients

2 sugar-free chocolate pudding snacks with 60 calories or less each
2 tablespoons reduced-fat creamy peanut butter
16 small square wonton wrappers
¼ cup Fat Free Reddi-wip

Optional topping: powdered sugar

Directions

To make the filling, in a medium bowl, gently swirl peanut butter into the pudding.

Lay a wonton wrapper flat on a dry surface. Place a little less than a tablespoon of filling (1/16th of the filling) in the center. Moisten all four edges by dabbing your fingers in water and going over the edges smoothly. Fold the bottom left corner to meet the top right corner, forming a triangle and enclosing the filling. Press firmly on the edges to seal.

Repeat with remaining wrappers and filling.

Bring a large skillet sprayed with nonstick spray to medium heat. Working in batches, place ravioli flat in the skillet, evenly spaced, and cook until slightly puffy, about 2 minutes per side. (Between batches, remove skillet from heat and re-spray.)

Just before serving, top each serving with a tablespoon of Reddi-wip, and enjoy!

MAKES 4 SERVINGS

157 calories per serving

For more recipes, tips & tricks, sign up for FREE daily emails at **hungry-girl.com!**

DESSERTS FOR ONE

CAKE MUGS & MORE
DESSERTS IN A MUG   10

Salted Caramel Chocolate Cake Mug

Chunky Monkey Cake Mug

So S'mores Cake Mug

Gooey German Chocolate Cake Mug

Coffee Cake in a Mug

Perfect Piña Colada Cake Mug

Strawberry Shortcake in a Mug

Oreo Cheesecake in a Mug

Apple Crisp in a Mug

Blueberry Crisp in a Mug

Peach Crisp in a Mug

Streusel-Topped Pumpkin Pie in a Mug

SOFTIES & WHOOPIE PIES   164

Freezy Cookies 'n Cream Whoopie Pie

Freezy Black Forest Whoopie Pie

Chill Out Choco-Coconut Whoopie Pie

Freezy-Cool Salted Caramel Whoopie Pie

Mr. Puffy Pumpkinhead Freezy-Cool
    Whoopie Pie

PB & Chocolate Chilly Whoopie Pie

FREEZY DESSERT SANDWICHES   194

The Triple-Chocolate Frost

Freezy PB S'mores Sandwich

Freezy Pretzel'wich Minis

Freezy PB Pretzel'wich Minis

Open-Faced PB-Caramel Bites

Open-Faced Chocolate-Peanut Freezies

ICE CREAM CUPCAKES
& OTHER FROZEN TREATS   208

Sweet 'n Salty Sundae Surprise

CRUNCHCAKES
& DESSERT CONES   256

Fruity Caramel Crunchcakes

TRIFLES, PARFAITS
& CRÈME BRÛLÉES   296

Key Lime Pie-fait

PB 'n Chocolate Puddin' Crunch Parfait

FRUITY FUN   316

Stuffed-Apple Apple Pie

Cherry-Picked Fake-Baked Apple

Pumpkin-Pie Apple Shakers

Sweet Cinnamon Pear Shakers

Stuffed-with-Love Strawberries

DESSERTS IN DISGUISE   334

DIY Choco-Mallow Coconut Nachos

DIY Banana & PB Nachos

DIY Cannoli Nachos

DIY Apple Pie Nachos

Crazy for Caramel Apple Pizza

Sassy S'mores Quesadilla

30 MINUTES OR LESS

The following recipes can be made and will be ready to enjoy in 30 minutes or less!

30 MINUTES OR LESS

These recipes can be made in 30 minutes or less, but you'll need to allow time for them to cool, chill, or freeze . . .

30 MINUTES OR LESS

5 INGREDIENTS OR LESS

5 INGREDIENTS OR LESS

CHOCOLATE MADNESS!

See also Cookies 'n Cream Dream, Red Velvet Revolution, Loco for Choco-Coconut, and More & More S'mores

CHOCOLATE MADNESS!

**CRUNCHCAKES &
DESSERT CONES**   256

Hideously Yummy Chocolate
   Caramel-PB Crunchcakes

Turtle Cheesecake Cones

**CREAM FLUFF CUPS,
CREAM FLUFF STACKS & MORE
DOUGH-BOTTOMED DESSERTS**   270

Mochaccino Cream Fluff Cups

Triple Chocolate Cream Fluffs

**TRIFLES, PARFAITS
& CRÈME BRÛLÉES**   296

PB 'n Chocolate Puddin' Crunch Parfait

FRUITY FUN   316

Stuffed-with-Love Strawberries

DESSERTS IN DISGUISE   334

DIY Cannoli Nachos

Dreamy PB Chocolate Ravioli Puffs

COOKIES 'N CREAM DREAM

**CAKE MUGS & MORE
DESSERTS IN A MUG**   10

Oreo Cheesecake in a Mug

CAKES & CHEESECAKES   90

Cookies 'n Cream Cake

BROWNIES & FUDGE   118

Cookies 'n Cream Brownies

SOFTIES & WHOOPIE PIES   164

Freezy Cookies 'n Cream Whoopie Pie

**ICE CREAM CUPCAKES
& OTHER FROZEN TREATS**   208

Freezy Cookies 'n Cream Scoop Sundaes

**CRUNCHCAKES &
DESSERT CONES**   256

Cookies 'n Cream Cones

RED VELVET REVOLUTION

CAKE POPS   64
Roarin' Red Velvet Cake Pops

CAKES & CHEESECAKES   90
Red Velvet Coconut Cream Cake

BROWNIES & FUDGE   118
Yum Yum Red Velvet Brownie Muffins

SOFTIES & WHOOPIE PIES   164
Mini Red Velvet Cheesecake
   Whoopie Pies

**ICE CREAM CUPCAKES
& OTHER FROZEN TREATS**   208
Mini Red Velvet Ice Cream Cakes

**TRIFLES, PARFAITS
& CRÈME BRÛLÉES**   296
Rockin' Red Velvet Trifle

LOCO FOR CHOCO-COCONUT

**CAKE MUGS & MORE
DESSERTS IN A MUG**   10
Gooey German Chocolate Mug

CAKE POPS   64
Coconut Patty Cake Pops

CAKES & CHEESECAKES   90
Red Velvet Coconut Cream Cake

BROWNIES & FUDGE   118
Crazy for Coconut Fudge

PIES & CUTIE PIES   142
Scoopy Mocha-Coconut Cream Pie

SOFTIES & WHOOPIE PIES   164
Chill Out Choco-Coconut Whoopie Pie

CRUNCHERS & CRUNCHETTES   228
German Chocolate Crunchers

DESSERTS IN DISGUISE   334
DIY Choco-Mallow Coconut Nachos

MORE & MORE S'MORES

PEANUT BUTTER PASSION

CARAMEL CRAZY

VERY VANILLA

CUPCAKES   28
Tie-Dye-For Cupcakes
Very Vanilla Fluffcakes
Vanilla Latte Cupcakes

CAKES & CHEESECAKES   90
Vanilla Caramel Dream Cake

SOFTIES & WHOOPIE PIES   164
Vanilla-licious Oatmeal Softies

**ICE CREAM CUPCAKES
& OTHER FROZEN TREATS**   208
Freezy Vanilla Cupcakes
Brownie-Bottomed Ice Cream Cake
Vanilla Sundae Scoops
Sweet 'n Salty Sundae Surprise
Very Vanilla Baked Alaska

**CREAM FLUFF CUPS,
CREAM FLUFF STACKS & MORE
DOUGH-BOTTOMED DESSERTS**   270
Vanilla Cream Fluff Cups

SAY CHEESECAKE

CUPCAKES   28
Double-Decker Fudgy
   Cheesecake Cupcakes
PB Cheesecake Chocolate Cupcakes

CAKES & CHEESECAKES   90
Banana Split Cheesecake
Super-Strawberry Cheesecake
Strawberry Upside-Down
   Cheesecake Squares
Chocolate Chip Candy Cane
   Cheesecake
Grasshopper Cheesecake
Mini PB&J Cheesecakes

BROWNIES & FUDGE   118
Swirly Chocolate-Cheesecake Brownies

SOFTIES & WHOOPIE PIES   164
Mini Red Velvet Cheesecake
   Whoopie Pies

CRUNCHERS & CRUNCHETTES   228
Blueberry Cheesecake Crunchers
Peaches & Cream Cheesecake
   Crunchers

**CRUNCHCAKES
& DESSERT CONES**   256
Turtle Cheesecake Cones

FRUITY & FABULOUS

See also Apple-mania, Strawberry Shortcake Surprise, Bananarama, Tropical Treats, and Pumpkin Attack!

APPLE-MANIA

STRAWBERRY SHORTCAKE SURPRISE

CAKE MUGS & MORE
DESSERTS IN A MUG   10
Strawberry Shortcake in a Mug

CRUNCHCAKES
& DESSERT CONES   256
Strawberry Shortcake Cones

CREAM FLUFF CUPS,
CREAM FLUFF STACKS & MORE
DOUGH-BOTTOMED DESSERTS   270
Strawberry Shortcake Cream Fluff Cups
Strawberry Shortcake Cream Fluff Stacks

DESSERTS IN DISGUISE   334
Strawberry Shortcake Waffle Tacos

BANANARAMA

CAKE MUGS & MORE
DESSERTS IN A MUG   10
Chunky Monkey Cake Mug

CUPCAKES   28
Banana Split Cuppycakes

CAKES & CHEESECAKES   90
Banana Split Cheesecake

BROWNIES & FUDGE   118
PB Banana Brownies

PIES & CUTIE PIES   142
PB & Banana Cream Pie
Banana Cream Cutie Pies

SOFTIES & WHOOPIE PIES   164
Banana Nut Softies

FREEZY DESSERT SANDWICHES   194
Chocolate Banana Freezy Sandwiches
Freezy Choco-Caramel Banana Bites

ICE CREAM CUPCAKES
& OTHER FROZEN TREATS   208
Freezy Downside-Up PB-Nana Dream Pie
Banana Split Pie

CRUNCHERS & CRUNCHETTES   228
Banana Split Crunchers

CREAM FLUFF CUPS,
CREAM FLUFF STACKS & MORE
DOUGH-BOTTOMED DESSERTS   270
Banana Cream Fluff Cups
Bananas Foster Cream Fluff Cups

DESSERTS IN DISGUISE   334
Banana Split Waffle Tacos
DIY Banana & PB Nachos

TROPICAL TREATS

PUMPKIN ATTACK!

There you have it . . . **200 delicious HG-rific desserts** that contain less than **200 calories each**. SWEET! 'Til next time, HAPPY CHEWING . . .

INDEX